The
Essence
of
Martial Arts

The Essence of Martial Arts

Making Your Skills Work in Practice

John Hennessy

iUniverse, Inc.
Bloomington

The Essence of Martial Arts
Making Your Skills Work in Practice

iUniverse books may be ordered through booksellers or by contacting:

iUniverse
1663 Liberty Drive
Bloomington, IN 47403
www.iuniverse.com
1-800-Authors (1-800-288-4677)

ISBN: 978-1-4620-5815-0 (sc)
ISBN: 978-1-4620-5816-7 (hc)
ISBN: 978-1-4620-5817-4 (ebk)

Library of Congress Control Number: 2011960052

Printed in the United States of America

iUniverse rev. date: 12/23/2011

Contents

This book is dedicated to Xuyi, who knows why,
to Coco (whose memory endures) and to Angel,
Gui-Gui and Java, who bring happiness to me every single day.

It is also dedicated to those who strive to understand
the essence of martial arts.

Introduction

In writing a book on martial arts, I would like to make clear from the offset that it does not pretend to discuss, debate, or deal with everything relating to every single martial art. There are just too many, the world over. Not to mention the subset of styles that each art has.

This book then, focuses mainly on those arts I have studied for a huge part of my life. So, it will deal with Tai Ji Quan (Tai Chi), Karate, Jeet Kune Do, and Gongfu (Kung Fu).

It is also clear that I will be writing from *my* perspective, with my own experience forming the basis of what is written. Nowhere here should any word be taken to endorse one style over another. It is simply, what it is, a record of my understanding of these martial arts.

It is also a labour of love. Martial arts should never be viewed as boring, as a chore. It is something I am fiercely passionate about. I don't pretend to be the best fighter, instructor, or even martial artist. I am just someone who trained very hard over the years and wanted to put the many thoughts in my head into a concise volume.

Another reason for doing this book is as a legacy for my students, as it is not really possible to cover in lesson time what I need to say.

It is my hope that many of you will take it for what it is, a concise collection of theories that I know to work in practise.

So, here it is. It may not be everyone's cup of tea, but I have been told that I have inspired countless students over the last twenty years, and it is my hope that this book will help to inspire some more of you.

Maybe you are a budding martial artist. Or you could be an extremely experienced martial artist. Or perhaps you are a student somewhere on the way to the first real standard, a black belt or sash. Who knows? Perhaps you've never been to a dojo, dojang or kwoon, and you are just interested in perhaps reading this book.

Note the title is called 'The Essence of Martial Arts' which means that it is not really possible for one book to contain all knowledge on all martial arts.

There are so many styles out there, so the focus here is on ones which I have studied to what I feel is a decent enough standard. Each has its own chapter on Tai Ji Quan (Tai Chi Chuan), Karate, Jeet Kune Do and Kung Fu.

My knowledge on these, and the information I wish to impart could easily fill one book each, or perhaps several volumes. I hope to do these books at some point.

To give you some background to this:-

I have studied Karate since 1986. My formal training began in 1989 and I achieved my first black belt in 1995. In 2007, I achieved the 3rd Dan level.

My Kung Fu training began in 1991 and with mainly personal training and guidance I achieved my black sash in Wing Chun in 1996.

With Jeet Kune Do and Tai Chi there are no formal belt systems and for Schools that run such a system, that is fine, but for me, I view both Arts as an ongoing journey. They are just too big and too varied to ever say I am a master in them.

I was first introduced to Tai Chi by Sifu Li in the early 1990s, but didn't really approach it formally until the year 2000. With Yang style I have learned up to the 103 Long Form, and many weapons forms in the system.

My Jeet Kune Do training began in 1995. I felt having done reasonably well learning Wing Chun Kung Fu I could try something similar, but new, also. With Wing Chun being the very foundation of Jeet Kune Do, it seemed a natural progression to me.

That is not to say this book is a watered down version. Far from it. It is short and to the point for a very good reason. A good martial artist or someone new to it will be able to pick up the elements quickly and put them to use, as many of my students have already.

So jump right in. Start at the start, or read the chapter you think will have most relevance to you, and your training. I have a lot to say, in some respects. But I want to guard against this book appearing too bloated, or saying the same things over and over again but with different words. This book hacks away the 'fat' so only the essentials, the *essence*, is left.

I was never naturally talented at martial arts, I just spent a lot of time trying to perfect the moves. That is all I did, and all anyone else can do. It's not difficult to achieve excellence in martial arts if you absolutely commit to doing so.

Finally, I have many people to thank, for where I am today. So I'll begin, and thank you in advance for opening yourself up to my way of thinking.

John Hennessy, October 2009-October 2011

1

Martial Arts Beginnings

Why I got into it, and how I began my formal training.

i). The Reasons Why I Got Into Martial Arts.

Why would anyone want to learn martial arts? Although easy to start with, it is very hard to master, the dedication required to achieve a good standard is more than many people can take. There is a misconception that it is all about violence, and that those who do it are aggressive too. Surely there are better things to do with your time and money?

There is, however, in today's world, here in the 21st century, a real need for martial arts, and for people to learn it, and to learn it well.

The good news is, it is often very enjoyable to learn and become good at a particular style of martial art that suits you.

Whichever style you choose, if you stick at it, it will become more to you than just a series of movements, kicks, blocks and punches. It becomes something that you find you almost cannot do without—it gets in your blood. I'd like to tell you why I got into martial arts.

I am not really talking about obsession here. I believe in martial arts from a practical viewpoint. I really believe that people need to know some form of self defence that will help them if they find themselves in a situation of real danger, where they or a loved one (or someone they see being attacked) could be seriously or fatally injured.

There is no guarantee in the world that would protect you from such an injury, but the likelihood is, someone who practices martial arts is more likely to walk away alive—and that is the key point—alive and able to walk home that night. A lot more likely than someone who does not have the skills to defend themselves or confidence gained from those skills to find a safe resolution to that situation.

You might think that because I have written this book that I have always been confident and always known exactly what to do in any given situation. You might even think that martial arts exponents may be something like the masters in the Kung Fu movies, able to do death defying moves at lightning speeds. In some cases, there are people who have studied martial arts for so long and have been so dedicated that they can do some very special things with their bodies.

For me, however, the road to martial arts was not an easy one, and perhaps more difficult for me than others. I did not arrive into this world a natural-born fighter, nor was I that naturally talented. In fact, fighting was something I largely disliked. I could not really understand why someone would want to use his or her limbs in such a manner as to hurt someone.

My mom and godmother were great role models for me. I had been brought up to respect others, especially those older than me, or other authority figures.

It began when I attended my Secondary school. I was aged just eleven and had thoroughly enjoyed my time at Junior school. Going to a much bigger place, with more students, teachers and of course, subjects I was rather overwhelmed and I suppose in that respect I was not alone.

While contemplating all that may have seemed difficult enough for an eleven-year-old, I was up for it and felt I was becoming more grown up. My mother and godmother had brought me up extremely well and I remain to this day thankful for their guidance. It was this that gave me a lot of courage to face this difficult transition from junior to senior school. I had made many friends there and none were coming to my new school.

I had hoped on my first day that I would make new friends, although I was aware that I was not much of a mixer, and so, I didn't make new friends easily.

Perhaps some of the more bullish children picked up on this and soon enough, for reasons to this day I find hard to explain, I became one of those children who found themselves getting 'picked on'. This would range from name-calling (I was told to ignore that by teachers because 'words don't hurt' which of course is not true, it is hurtful) to actual physical challenges which some of you will be familiar with 'I'll see you at the school gates at home-time'.

For some, they didn't wait for home-time and the fights would start in the playground, or on other occasions before, during and after lessons and maybe when I would be walking to the bus stop, which was close to a mile away from the school.

It seemed a very surreal experience. I didn't understand why they were attacking me, or why I could not seem to muster up a suitable response. I had told teachers what had happened because I had been told that was the right thing to do. In fact, it only served to make things much much worse and I continued to have these surreal experiences. In my mind, I was doing nothing that made these kids want to attack me, but I was also doing nothing wrong by telling the teachers I was actually being physically hurt as a result of these encounters.

Even back then, I do recall that while punches and kicks and slaps and chops would hurt, they seemed to lose their effectiveness or potency rather quickly, and I then assumed perhaps they would stop their assaults. Usually that would actually be the case, until the next new school day, and it would begin all over again.

I was pretty bright in most of the classes, and really excelled in some subjects. I felt that if the teacher would give me more attention in class, ask me questions, or get me to work in groups or to partner up, I would get more respect from classmates, and I suppose to a certain extent, I did. And so, they would move on to someone else to focus their energies on.

There were still a few kids there who seemed to just have one sole purpose to their existence—to make my life a misery. And for two years, it was certainly the case. I hated the school—*that* school.

I thought the teachers were worse than useless, because telling them what was happening would turn around to the point that they would ask me why I thought I was being attacked. Instead of dragging these kids into detention or suspending them, I found that I would be the one staying after school in detention!

Given that I had had threats like 'I'll see you at the school gates at 3:30' come all too often, maybe detention was the teachers' indirect way of keeping me safe.

This couldn't go on, of course, and during the summer of 1986 I resolved to find out all I could about martial arts. I had seen films like *The Karate Kid* and whilst I thought the film itself was pretty poor with a completely improbable climax, I did relate to what the main protagonist was going through.

What I didn't have, unlike Danny LaRusso in the film, was a local martial arts master to teach me how to deal with these 'children' effectively.

So I would mimic what he did in the film, practising kicks for a few hours a day and I did start to feel I was getting stronger. But I knew kicks on their own wouldn't be enough.

With no local martial arts master on hand, I considered joining classes. What I saw of them though really put me off. I would go to clubs, and peep through the windows to see what was going on, and what was actually going on? People, being thrown across the room. People shouting loudly at each other. People, punching and kicking each other. *Hard.* I did't like the look of it at all, much less fancy joining a class, and paying for it so that someone could do that to me.

Options were few and time was running out. The summer holidays of 1986 would be over in just a month, and I would be starting my third year at that hellish school. Oh yes, it would have been possible to get transferred to another school, but quite likely I would meet the same sort of kids there. Or maybe something worse.

In the cold light of day I realised it was just a handful of people who were causing me problems. I felt if I could just stand up to them, maybe their over- confidence would be exposed, and that in itself would give me confidence.

Many years later, I would understand that size, gender, body type would not really matter in terms of how you fight them. The tactics, in how you approach them, might have to be adapted, but the strategy, that is to roundly defeat your opponent, would always be the right one.

However, this was 1986, and I had to quickly get some skills together. I doubted I could be a black belt in Karate in just five weeks as in *The Karate Kid.* I had just three weeks left, and had just two kicks in my repertoire . . . a front kick and a roundhouse kick.

I didn't count the side kick, it seemed far from good enough anyway and also, the front kick had been used on me a number of times. I actually wanted to spend some time on learning how to block it effectively.

I was in town and I think I had been to see a film at the local cinema, when I went into a bookstore and happened across a book on Karate, *Step by Step Karate* by Vic Charles.

I read a few pages and decided that it would be a good buy for me. It had good pictures and concepts seemed to be pretty well explained.

This was the third option I was looking for. Of course, I would have loved it if I had known someone who could teach me to protect myself – not so much to fight, I wasn't interested in that . . . but the book would be money well spent and time well invested if I could make it work.

On return to School that Autumn I felt more confident. I had no idea why, I just felt like I could actually defend myself better than I had in the last two years.

Within a week it started. Only against one particular person. He was the year 'tough' and most people in my year feared him. He was tall, and had a mean look about him. He had been particularly vicious to me in years one and two but wanted to take it up a notch.

In the class, I had arrived a bit later than the others but grabbed a stool and went to sit down. This guy grabbed the stool and I nearly fell off. He was freakishly strong.

However, I wasn't taking his nonsense this time and did my best to wrestle the stool from him. Then he hit me in the chest, extremely hard.

It's fair to say I hadn't been hit that hard in my life before. But prior to that day, I may have hit the ground due to the force. This time, I kept my balance—score one for the power of martial arts!

I managed to overcome him using some of the skills I have been learning, but suffice to say, I never got bothered by him again, and for the most part it was a good thing, as no-one else really bothered me either. I did not become 'the bully as a result of being bullied', I just went about things in my quiet way, and focussed on my lessons in my remaining time at school, and that is what I encourage any young person reading this book to do so too.

ii). How I Began My Formal Training.

It would be a full three years before I would start formal training with a real martial arts instructor. It was 1989 and I was now leaving the school that had given me so many problems with good grades, and a feeling that I would be leaving much more confident than when I had entered five years before.

Martial arts, in my limited understanding of them, had helped to give me a 'centre' and sense of balance in my teenage years. If I had not started training in 1986 I have no doubt I would have failed most, if not all of my exams, which would have been devastating to me.

I did feel I really was ready for formal training now. I know some people say 'I wish I had started this when I was five years old'. Perhaps all of us share this view, but you are never too old to learn, and to start later is better than not starting at all, and wondering what might have been achieved.

In 'Acknowledgements', at the end of this book, I pay tribute to the teachers I have had over the time. Special mention is given here to my first instructor, as she was the one who has influenced me the most.

Sifu Miss Karen Li-Kung Fu and Karate Instructor from 1989 -1991 (at the School) and 1991-1996 on a 1-2-1 personal training level.

Karen Li was my first real instructor. Karen was just 18 when I first enrolled on one of her Karate classes, because she taught them when her father was unavailable. At that time, she already held a 1st Dan black belt in Karate and also Judo. Almost needless to say she was a expert in Kung Fu and had practised many styles, mainly Wing Chun, but also Shaolin, Lau Gar, Choy Li Fut and Hung Gar Kung Fu.

She was a 'qi gong' student also. I didn't really understand it at the time, I wish I had done so. But how can you really understand all that a master can impart to you? I was too young, and far too inexperienced at that time. Like most foolish young people, I thought I was better than I really was. I mean, I was okay, I had a decent grasp of skills. But I wasn't a tenth as good as the fighter in my mind's eye.

Karen Li, on the other hand, was the 'real deal' and was *extremely* skillful. I don't think, even to this day, I have seen anyone move with such grace and yet such power.

This came about because the Karate and judo classes were more popular for some reason. She always rated Kung Fu above Karate and Judo, although understood the benefits of the systems.

One day, I think it was my 600th lesson or something (I used to train 4-6 times a week), on this occasion, no-one else turned up. Only me. I thought the lesson would not go ahead. To Karen's credit, she began the lesson as she began all others. I said it was not necessary to go ahead but she insisted, saying 'we always teach those ready to learn', and that the fact that I was the only one there made no difference.

But it did. I felt special, but also very nervous. You see, Karen Li was a tremendous martial artist and most of the other students, including me, were in awe of her.

So this lesson was going to be a bit different. There was to be no hiding from Karen, or her training method - as I would find out later, which would be relentless and bordering on torture. But to simplify her teaching like that would be disingenuous. Her teaching was extremely effective and I use what methods she taught me to this day.

Her training methods were 'different', shall we say. She had a garden in which she did a lot of her training. She introduced me to 'the block' which was to be my best friend. All I saw was a stone bench from which bits of jagged stone protruded, which she explained could be raised to different heights and had multiple uses.

So the first lesson was to learn how to strike, and hard. Without the need for using heavy weights or dubious cardio-vascular routines, after two hours hitting this stone table my fingers, hands, even my arms were shaking.

When I asked her why I had to do this (when I had actually thought I had come to learn Kung Fu) she said that this was not the time for questions. She also pointed out I was wasting time by asking the question. But she said, in her self deprecating manner 'I'll humour you. The only question you need to ask yourself is 'How good at Kung Fu do I really want to be?'

I soon learned that this question, if you replace the words 'Kung Fu' with whatever you are looking to do with your life, was a lesson for your life. And this is what I was taught in the very first one-to-one lesson.

That is not to say that is how I do one-to-one lessons. This is because her teaching methods became increasingly more extreme when say a tournament neared (more on that later).

By a private lesson, I thought she meant an hour. More than six hours later, I'm still there, being put through all manner of kicks, punches, blocks, forms, and exercises that bordered on torture. In fact I think it was torture, dressed up as personal training.

I was close to passing out, when we stopped. I hadn't even noticed her father had returned some hours earlier. But he seemed to be looking out from the window, half smiling, half resigned (as if to say 'this boy is not tough enough for training in Chinese Kung Fu'). At that point, I'd have agreed with him. In fact, I would have agreed with anything to get out of there.

It was like the Karen I thought I knew at the club had been kidnapped and been replaced by this incredibly harsh person. I wanted to ask 'Who are you, really, and what have you done with her?' but I had already asked one question today. I figured if I wanted to get out of there, I had best keep my mouth shut.

'Okay then' she said as I was going 'see you at 6am tomorrow. We go for a run'.

I was thinking, 'What??? Is she kidding me?'

She must have read my face. 'If we stop training now, we lose everything we've done. You don't strike me as a quitter. So then, I will see you at 6am tomorrow. Don't be late.'

It's a curious thing, pain. Practically every part of my body was sending signals to my brain as if to say 'Now you know what a workout is. You've never done one in your life, until today.'

It's true. I figured I lost half my body weight in that one session.

The next morning I somehow managed to get there for the run. I imagined we'd set off jogging on the road, but as Karen didn't live too far from Sutton Park we soon diverted to there. She set quite a pace. I knew she was fit, but had never actually seen her run. She went off like a bullet. Maybe not that fast, but close. I was thinking how muddy my trainers and clothes were getting. She was having none of it, saying 'Sure. Focus on that, and you will be caught and beaten by your assailants, buried under some rotting tree here in the park, and that will be 'you'.'

Funny how harsh criticism can sometimes spur you on. I chased after her as fast as I could, but still couldn't catch up. It would take me a full two years to outrun her, but even then I'm sure she was slowing down just to help me.

It is fair to say I didn't like her much during the training. I thought she was far too harsh and critical, and more often I felt demoralised than inspired. I thought her methods were brutal and were more in keeping with torture than real martial arts.

I realised though, she was being excessively hard for a reason. I was in no way an exceptional fighter—quite the reverse, actually. I could take punishment but could not really bear to give it out. To hit another human being would almost make me physically sick, something which through necessity I learned to change over the years. To be soft on me, to say 'it's alright, leave it for another day' would have been totally counter productive.

Her Wing Chun and overall Wushu abilities remain the best I have had the privilege to see, and I was delighted to have stayed the course. I am sure there are other many good Wing Chun teachers who can teach the technical aspects of the Art to a great standard, but few who would match up to her style and effectiveness.

As I spent most of my formulative training with Karen Li, it is probably more appropriate to write a separate book on this, which is a future intention of mine.

2

Basics

No grasp of the fundamentals hastens your defeat.

Chapter focus: *In this chapter I am offering martial artists specific pointers that will help them in their practise. I believe the items in this chapter to be suitable for those new to martial arts training, but also to those well advanced in their styles.*

The chapter is about the fundamentals—the real core things you need to know, and secondly the things that teachers do not spend time telling you.

Some of it may seem all too obvious, but in my experience even some of the best fighters, and some of my students forget the basics in the heat of the moment. That is why I state that without a firm grasp of the fundamentals, a fighter is on the way to defeat.

You may think yourself well versed on what is to follow. I hope you will read it again and again to make sure you have taken it all in.

*   *   *

To guard the centre is to be in the right place at the right time, for both attack and defence.

*   *   *

Failure to protect the centre offers an invitation to attack and easily be defeated.

*   *   *

Keep it simple. Flashy techniques may look good on camera, but the truth is they rarely work in the real world. For this reason, engage your opponent by making contact with the appropriate measure of distance, break his defence by 'sticking' to him, and break his guard, hitting hard and fast.

*   *   *

If you turn your back, get cornered, close your eyes (even for a second), or simply back off, this is a sure and certain way to lose—a fight, a tournament, your life.

*   *   *

The right approach is to engage your adversary 'ahead' of him—be first, be fastest, be hardest.

*   *   *

Do not get caught up in the rituals of showing too much respect to your opponent. You will show disrespect to your Art if you do this. There is no honour, and no point in losing 'honourably'.

No opponent is unbeatable. If you think you will lose just because he wears a higher belt than you, you WILL lose. Let your skill dictate what will happen in a fight. If you lose, you lose, but don't let your 'thinking' predict what will happen.

*   *   *

If your skill *is* good enough, you will prevail, but do not cloud your thinking, and hasten your defeat, by contemplating the 'what if's'.

*   *   *

To fight force with force is folly. If your opponent is bigger and naturally stronger than you, how can you expect to fight him like for like? Exploit his weaknesses, because he will have them.

*   *   *

Do not think because your opponent is weaker / shorter / smaller than you, that it will be an easy victory. If anything, it will be harder. Treat all opponents the same—with respect—but do not think that he is just another fighter—you must continually assess what is happening during the fight in order to beat him.

*   *   *

If you have an opponent on the run, finish him. Do not give him a second to breath or recover. To do so gives him a chance. Do not give him that chance.

* * *

Do not 'think' during a fight. <u>You do not have the time</u>. The time for thinking is before the fight, not during. You just have to let your 'tools' do their job. Don't ever get confused about that.

* * *

If an opponent is good with high kicks, you need to reduce the distance between you and him in order to stop him being able to kick. If you give him space, expect him to exploit that.

* * *

In the same way, if an opponent is good with kicks below the waist, you must use an appropriate measure of distance in order to deal with him. In addition, you can use a 'stop-kick' or heel kick to neutralise his attack.

* * *

Many people rush in instead of actually having a game plan beforehand. So what happens, against an opponent who is superior to you (hand to hand) is that you get hit, many times, unnecessarily so. That's not even good if you are used to taking hits. Invite and draw out the attack by all means, but use an effective counter.

* * *

Don't just use your blocking arm to merely 'block'. Let me explain that. What I mean is, the block is not the final act of the arm technique, rather, it is the beginning. Use the block in such a way that allows you to follow on or through to the next technique, which, if you have the correct position on the opponent, allows you to hit him. If you don't use your block in this way, you will miss countless opportunities to counter strike.

* * *

Your punch is your 'lead-in' to hit your opponent with the ability to hit him quickly, and withdraw it quickly into the guard arm position. Don't leave it out there for him to grab.

* * *

Don't merely accept that your opponent beat you, or can beat you, simply because of his hand speed. He can be as fast as lightning but if he cannot land a shot on you due to how you move and defend, well, what of his speed then? Does it matter? The real reason an opponent will beat you is because he is more accurate and has a better sense of timing than you, and speed is just one factor, technique and power are the other factors.

* * *

Are your legs strong? Do you know how to stand? Do you understand how to shift your body weight? Do you know how to position yourself so that you can be in the best place to attack your opponent, whilst at the same time keep your optimum defence? If you cannot answer 'yes' to these questions, you lack the basics for fighting. Let's look at each in turn.

Are your legs strong? This may sound obvious, but without strength from 'the ground up' you will be defeated by an opponent with a better stance, and understanding of stances and positioning than you. Legs get strong through practising stances, and later, through conditioning on the wooden dummy.

Let's say you do not possess or intend to get a wooden dummy (for whatever reason, including the possibility you do not want to learn Wing Chun). You still need to have strong legs. A strong stance provides the root from which any technique you demonstrate will succeed. In the same way, if you do not spend enough time working on your stance and body position, then you are already sowing the seeds of your defeat.

If you don't practise long and hard on this, you won't be able to defeat an opponent. He will simply sweep your legs away and you will not be able to regain a suitable fighting position from the ground. Stay on your feet if you want to win.

The best way to practise this is via the 'ma-bo' or *horse-stance*. Standing straight but also relaxed and alert, move the left leg to the side and the right leg to the side, then sit or squat as low as you can. It is not meant to be comfortable so if you don't feel enough strain on the legs, especially the thighs, then try and stretch and bend a lot lower until you can. Then hold the position for three, six, twelve minutes, and longer. The longer you can hold the position the stronger your legs, your balance, and ultimately *you* will be.

Do you know how to stand?

Again, this may sound obvious, but usually people think they have a good stance until they are shown to the differ. In some cases, whereby you are not fighting an opponent, such lack of attention to detail would be okay. But if you are up against someone, and you show a poor attention to your stance, they will overwhelm you, and quickly.

Do you understand how to shift your body weight?

Such an understanding is critical to your remaining balance and being able to defend and attack with power and precision. It is vital to have a low centre of gravity, and from that position, be able to 'shift' position to the right or left side, but also forward and back (or even with an angular position) without over-balancing.

You need to put your whole body behind a technique in order for it to be successful. This means that, if we are talking about punching techniques, that the 'punch' itself (or if a leg technique, the 'leg' itself) should be the last thing you should be thinking about, or making happen. By 'making it happen' I mean, if you plan to do a kick, sometimes, when it is poorly executed, the shifting of balance (important to get the body behind the kick) is forgotten about. In addition, other components of a kick can be missed with poor execution. It is only when you really break it down that you see just how much you are missing out on.

Why take such an exhaustive look at something that takes a split second to do?

Well, the sum of the parts, complete the whole. The kick is the end product, but it is how you get to do that perfect execution of the kicking technique . . . it is that what makes the journey to that standard worthwhile.

Do you know how to position yourself so that you can be in the best place to attack your opponent, whilst at the same time keep your optimum defence?

If your opponent is too far away when you plan your attack (or counter-attack) then it will fail. Knowing how to stand, shift your body weight, and taking up the best position to allow an advantageous attack is what you need to do. Every time.

If he moves, stick with him. Do not allow him the opportunity to move away from you. Don't allow him breathing space. Keep pressure on him constantly by closing his space down, and varying your attacks. This is a strategy which has always worked for me.

Closing chapter notes: *You don't have to over-complicate things! You must know that you don't need a thousand moves to defeat an opponent. You may only need one, if the attack / counter-attack is placed well enough. Think about it for a second. Of course it is better to know a whole range of moves and not need to use them, as opposed to not knowing nearly enough moves, in order to stay safe.*

3

Exercises for the Body

Focussing purely on skill training alone is a pointless endeavour.

Chapter focus: *In this chapter, we'll look at exercises you can do that will not only supplement your training, but enhance it also.*

There is so much emphasis on being fit and less on skill work, or there are other classes that do the opposite—all skill and little or no exercise.

Some martial arts require a lot of flexibility, others less so.

What is really required, like most things in life, is a sense of balance.

Don't ever spend too much time on one aspect at the expense of another. Give it the time, energy and balance that it deserves.

Have you ever been in a class whereby you may have been expected to warm up on your own, beforehand? I have, and cannot think of a potentially more dangerous exercise—or lack of exercise . . . or quicker way to get a serious injury.

The effective warm-up is essential. Many students forego a good warm-up, and some think if the warm-up is too long, that it eats into the main part of the lesson.

Sometimes the class will begin with the words 'protections on!!' and this means you have the best part of the next hour in sparring. Whilst the main part of the exercises you will be doing are okay in themselves, you will be at a disadvantage if you have not warmed up sufficiently. The main problems you will experience are shortness of breath, and a lack of elasticity or flexibility in your hips.

How long the warm-up actually is depends on a number of factors:-

Weather: If training out-side, and it is cold, a longer, more vigorous warm-up is required. But all warm-ups should start with gentle exercises, moving steadily to increasingly difficult ones. You should never start vigorous training like doing high or fast kicking techniques from 'cold'. Warm up properly, and put effort into stretching, taking care to do it properly and safely. Don't kid yourself you have stretched if you haven't done so. An eight to ten minute warm-up including stretching of the limbs, plus an aerobic / anaerobic workout will suffice.

If it is hot, or the sun is bearing down on you then you may feel you don't need an extensive warm-up, but you would be wrong. Of course, you still need to warm up, but perhaps concentrate more on stretching than the more strenuous routines that get you to perspire heavily, because, as it is hot, you will get to sweat quite a lot anyway.

Caution: If training outside you may need some form of sun-block in order to protect yourself from sunburn. This is no joke in some countries where you can have a 'low' sun in the summer, and the chance of sunburn and even heatstroke are very high.

The type of training involved:

If you are doing a gentle art, say Tai Chi, then gentle exercises throughout are called for. You can exercise gently for five to ten minutes and be secure in the knowledge that these exercises prepare you for the form work, applications, or *qigong,* that lies ahead.

For Tai Chi, start with your heels together, standing straight, and be alert but relaxed.

Place one foot to the side, pointing the toes, then gently place the rest of the foot down, flat and secure on the surface. Then do the same with the other foot. This gives you a secure, stable stance from which to start any exercise including the first basic form.

Basic exercises:

Arm circles inner / outer (with breathing)
Shoulder circles / forward and back
Elbow raises
Knee bends
Knee bends—circular
Groin stretch
Elbow pull in—in front, behind head, lower back

Wrist circles
Finger linking / rotation
Jogging on the spot
Heels back and feet high off ground
Moving side to side—keep feet together
Move back and forth—keep feet together
One leg in front, then change with the other as above, but add swinging
    arms
Move leg behind crossed behind you, the in front as above plus arm
    circle—inner and outer
Groin stretch—second round
Shoulder width—arm / wrist stretch, left, right and centre.

Additional:

Floor exercises.

Knees forward, sit on backs of heels, place hands behind you and raise left
then the right hips, then raise centre together.

Place one leg in front and place in flat on the floor, as much as it will go.
Try not to let the knee bend, keep the leg straight.

Reach forward with one hand and try to reach the toes. If not, place hand
against the outside of the leg and hold. Do not 'bounce'.

Bring the leg back and replace it with the other leg, then repeat the steps
above.

Place both hands in front and place one knee down in front of you.
With the other leg, place straight and to the side at a 90 degree angle.

Rotate the waist to place one hand against the toes, and hold (do not
'bounce').

Leg strength and flexibility go together. No point being able to kick high
if you do not have sufficient power and strength in your legs.

Also, no good being powerful if you can't get your legs above stomach height—and be able to kick with real power, speed and focus.

A strong, developed, and toned stomach can help you take shots, if they get in during a fight. It may be the difference between getting winded, or perhaps suffer broken ribs and then going on to lose, or it could be that it helps you deal with what it coming at you effectively, and going on to win. So, as well as doing sit-ups, for which you can do three primary types;

    i) Straight lift and crunch the stomach (easy)
    ii) Lift and turn to the left and right, then crunch forward (intermediate)
    iii) As i) above, but slowly and controlled (hard)

Lie on your back and hold a training ball, away from your body. Push it up and down repeatedly, and, keeping your feet together, start to raise your legs off the floor, and keep them straight too. This will work the lower abdomen especially, and is one of the best core conditioning exercises that there is.

You can make it more difficult—and beneficial, by raising and lowering the legs at different heights. The hardest thing to do is to keep the legs off the floor, but also as close to the floor as possible.

Developing speed, power and flexibility takes time. Let's look at each in turn.

Speed

Use the kick bag or focus pads to ensure fast repetitions of leg techniques.

If you don't have use of such equipment, practise changing sharply from one leg to the other.

Rope work—whereby you skip rope for three minutes and then have a break—for a maximum of 30 seconds, is ideal for picking up leg speed, and speed increase overall. It is also one of the most ideal training methods to lose weight quickly, although you have to build up your fitness on it. There is no point in labouring to a 10 minute workout on the rope, when what is needed is a fast, up-tempo workout for a full three minutes. The ideal training set when doing rope work is where during your training you can do three minutes, three times. All efforts should be concentrated on achieving this level of fitness. The reason is, that if you can keep going for this period of time, at a high intensity and pace, you will have a pool of endurance to draw on. This can often be the dividing line between winning and losing a fight.

Power

Hit as hard as you can without overbalancing. Some people put everything into a single attack, thinking that through power, they can knock anything down. But should the same approach miss the intended target, what do you do then? How quick can you recover your defensive position? You cannot leave yourself open, even if you are able and willing to 'take shots'.

Also, ensure you have done a sufficient warm up before you start to kick with one kick after another. Your body has to warm up correctly first.

You can also increase power by switching stances quickly. Of course, the supporting leg must be placed correctly so that you can land sufficient power that will knock your opponent out. By combining speed with power with flexibility, you can hit your opponent several times, with speed, at different heights. This is the way to train, so that in the fight situation, you can be confident you have the tools to do the job effectively.

Pad work, hitting an opponent who has protective gear on, and also working on devices such as a wooden dummy all help to increase power. You'll know, because these training aids do manage to provide the resistance that you need in order that the things you apply in training, can be applied in practise.

Flexibility

Stretching, and repeated exercises to make your legs more flexible are vital for the all round martial artist. If you have poor flexibility it is simply something you cannot overlook.

Although quite painful, not to mention stressful on the joints of the legs, find—or construct a post where you can elevate your leg. This is best to attempt after a sufficient warm up has been done.

Shadow boxing is great for loosening the joints. Or gentle stretching is also good.

You can also use a chair—I have in training, this works well for me and my students.

Combine this by investing in, or obtaining use of, a flexibility-training band.

Metal leg stretchers are good, as are the ones in which you can sit in and turn the attached 'steering wheel' to enable your legs to open up to side splits, but the possibility of injury is rather high. I achieved the side splits aged eighteen with the help of my instructor, Sifu Li.

But the cost was high, as my legs were pushed to the side by concrete blocks placed on the inside part of my thighs and then pushed by my teacher to the side. Very painful indeed. I didn't walk properly for about two weeks, and passed out due to the pain. So it is not a recommended procedure.

If you want to improve your flexibility from quite a low level, it is important to recognise that if you push it too fast, too quickly, you may injure yourself, and then your ability to recover quickly will be hindered.

So, stretch as wide and as long as you can, and once the pain really starts, try hold it for between 15 and 30 seconds, but no more. Rest, and try the other leg or side, and do some knee bends in-between. You will be aiding your legs' recovery as well as making them more able to do wider / longer on the second and subsequent rounds.

The other worthwhile method is to buy a leg stretcher that will see two 'arms' placed against the inside of your legs, by the ankles. You pull the third 'arm' in towards you, and this allows the stretch to be maintained, and slowly, improved.

As you push it more and more, the pain of stretching increases. There needs to be a recovery period before attempting this again. Leave it for two or three days and then you can try again, and find you can stretch some more, for longer, and to a wider angle.

Serious injury can happen when attempting the splits if your body is not ready. Take appropriate care not to overdo this at first, and your ability to increase the range and subsequent kicking ability will be significantly enhanced, as will your recovery rate between sessions.

Further endurance training:

Use the area you train in to run backwards, distributing the weight evenly so as to keep on the balls of your feet.

As you move and get to each corner of the training area, turn sharply, keeping your blocking arm up and let go a flurry of punches. Then continue to move.

Press ups—including normal arm position and wide arm press-ups to build your upper arm strength are vital.

Combination Drill 1 (from Wing Chun Kung Fu System, First Syllabus)

There are many combination drills, such as the preliminary one I use in Kung Fu involves seven techniques. Utilise a natural stance, where your knees are slightly bent and do the following:-

    i)   Left Punch
    ii) Right Punch

iii) Left Bon Sao (Wing Block)
iv) Right Bon Sao
v) Strike with Right fist
vi) Left Punch,
vii) Right Heel Kick.

What it is used for: *A combination drill should be practised vigorously and regularly so that when it is unleashed, it has an intensity and variety which opponents will find hard to live with.*

Use variety in attack without disregarding your defence. This is what the combination drills are all about. Once an opponent has perhaps blocked your punching attack, the focus switches seamlessly to kicks, sweeps, or throwing attacks.

At the time of writing, there are thirty-eight combination drills in my Kung Fu system. All are varied and have their individual merits. All are effective at whatever level you are in the system, which means that you don't have to reach a black sash to be a great and effective fighter.

Training aides: Invest in, or again, get use of, the 'rattan rings'. This is an excellent training tool for the arms, because when you are in the *ma bo* or 'horse stance, you are building your leg strength, but by using the rattan rings (the simple bamboo ones are the best to try, at least until you get used to them) your arm strength multiplies also.

Leg raises are excellent for training the stomach and strengthening the abdomen. Keep at them because you never know when someone will slip your guard, and if you cannot take a hard shot, you will be going down.

Closing chapter notes: *A flexible, fit and skilled fighter will always win out against one who does not have a suitable understanding and experience of these things. That is not to say a less flexible fighter cannot win against one who is—that is not the point. The point is that the flexibility, fitness and skill of anyone can be improved and it is those elements, which you should focus on.*

4

Conditioning

Get the mind and body working as one. Good skills and ability on their own simply won't be good enough. Because, 'good enough', never is.

Chapter focus: *Conditioning in many people's minds means the conditioning of the body. Whilst it is a very important aspect, as seen in the previous chapter, your mind must also be conditioned.*

Without that, you are once again left to fight with only skill or luck to help you, and you may find it may not be enough.

Fighters do not win on skill alone. You must condition your body and also your mind to the task at hand, and the two must work together to produce the optimum result.

Over-confidence breeds cockiness and a quick defeat against a more skilled and experienced opponent.

If one is obsessed with getting a black belt / sash . . . then his whole martial arts life is a waste of time. You should actually see the journey *as* the goal . . . otherwise reaching the proverbial summit is pointless.

Belts really do not matter. **Read that again and again until it has gone in.** And while it is true that it is easy for those who have attained black belt level to say this, the real question is, can you do what you are supposed to do, when you need to do it? Do you think a belt will help you do that? It is no good being able to do it in a dojo, dojang or a kwoon. You have to be able to do it anywhere, anytime, anyhow.

Don't delude yourself that you are good just because you wear the colour black around your waist. It is good—a standard—and that is all. If the belt was not needed to keep the trousers up, should you really be wearing it at all?

Be humble—don't be a show-off. The true martial artist reveals himself in his every action. If you have to tell someone you do martial arts, you've actually lost the point, and their respect !

Lack of focus in martial arts means lack of focus in life. You cannot achieve anything without focus, self-determination and self-discipline.

Don't be concerned about getting hit. It won't be as bad as you think and if you are constantly worried about being hit, you will be!

Guard the centre. Guard the centre. Guard the centre. Make this the centre-piece of your training, in your thoughts and in your actions. If you cannot guard the centre, you will be defeated.

Attack the centre. Attack the centre. Attack the centre. Don't let your opponent off the hook for a second. By attacking the centre, you give him no chance to settle. He constantly has to be using his arms to block your punches or higher kicks. When he has to apply a block, you can cut him open by attacking the part of the centre that is now open. Be first, be fastest, be hardest.

Notes on Chain Drills and repetition of techniques:

Drills that involve repeating the same technique, again and again and again, often have student's brains turning off quickly by sending a message to the brain of 'I'm tired, and my arms are tired'.

The problem is that unless you apply yourself properly to the mundane repetitiveness of these drills—and try and enjoy them, you will give up at some point.

You may ask, 'Is there a way to make the drills more fun?' . . . well, to use a driving analogy, motorway driving is one of the most boring, mundane uses for your car. Unfortunately, if you want to get somewhere reasonably fast, you need the motorway, and a heady number of miles on it too, in order to get to your destination.

There are no traffic lights or pedestrians on the motorway, plus, you will just have to keep the car in a straight line for much of the journey until you have to turn off the motorway, even then, it is done by easing off on the left side of the carriageway.

There is not a lot for you to do. It is, well, boring.

However, the good driver will occupy his or her mind to keep the journey interesting.

In the same way, a good martial artist will never consider any particular task boring. It is, what it is, and so the literal translation of 'Kung Fu' being to 'work hard', then perhaps you can understand that whatever the task is, you do it to the absolute best of your ability.

How to make it fun, then? Or at least, *more* fun?

Punch Drills: These can tire you out extremely quickly. Therefore you need to do them to build up *stamina* and *resistance* which equals *endurance*.

Punches take a lot of power, focus, energy and co-ordination. Try to do a hundred or so punches from 'cold' and see how much your arms hurt after this exercise. Hurts rather bad, doesn't it? After that, you may not want to do any more punches, and perhaps you would not be blamed for thinking that.

To make it more fun, or at least bearable, focus on doing each technique cleanly and correctly. Check your body position and then, the height and position of the punch. Make sure you are not locking the arm out, and punch as fast and as hard as you can. Then repeat it. If you are doing an endurance test, like say 100, 500 or a thousand punches, then you need to check all the above at regular intervals.

Then your drills will become more fun. The natural result of which, you will do more of them and perfect your technique.

So, in building up the punching techniques so that repetitive movements are replaced by clear, focused ones, your punch drills become sharp.

Leg / kicking techniques:

Forms / Kata practise: With short forms, if done correctly, you will find them tiring. Don't be so quick to rush through the long ones either. You should enjoy each movement, and flow from one to the other. Karate and

Kung Fu forms do have momentary pauses but even so, it should be a movement without form, or more accurately 'formlessness within form'.

This should not mean you do what you want with the ancient forms. You should still stick to what you have been taught, and do each stance, arm or leg technique, short form or long form correctly.

Don't replace specific motions for generalised ones. That leads to lethargy, but strangely, the false belief that you are actually working hard ! No. Do it properly, or not at all. That is a rule for most, if not all things, in life.

The Wooden Dummy

Make sure you have an opportunity to use the wooden dummy. No serious martial artist, and specifically, no serious Kung Fu exponent can hope to develop his or her skills without wooden dummy training. In my school, all students condition themselves on the 'wooden man' . . . irrespective of what style they are learning.

Don't join a School / Club that doesn't have a wooden dummy (or similar training device).

If the instructor doesn't have one at the venue, ask if he has one himself—and could you have some private tuition with him on this. Then you know you have an instructor who treats Kung Fu training seriously.

Wooden Dummies are not cheap. At least—the good ones are not cheap. Don't buy anything second rate, you will regret it.

Spinning or Static Dummies—Which should you choose? If you can, train with both, but the former is much more flexible and realistic for your training.

At first, the dummy will hurt you. Persevere with it. You will get conditioned. But never think you are stronger than the Dummy. It always is stronger than you. Always !

As time goes on, you will be able to apply moves such as Bon Sao and Pak Sao more forcefully, and not risk injury, or even slight bruising.

The most classically known wooden dummy form is the 116 form, however it is not an easy form. In fact, if you have been taught Wing Chun Kung Fu properly, you won't learn the 116 form until you have completed the 'open hand' forms, of which there are three. In my system, you also learn four wooden dummy forms before attempting the 116 Form.

That is not to say Wing Chun does not have weapons forms. It does, but it is extremely important to do these aforementioned open hand forms in order. You can learn other Kung Fu forms in the meantime, but to attempt to use a wooden dummy to pull out techniques from the three forms would be unrealistic at best, and just plain wrong at worst.

The **Muk Yan Jong** ("wooden man / wooden dummy") is used to practice flowing from one position or technique to another without losing contact with the opponent.

Many of the elements of the Wooden Man form are closely related in application to the Third Form, although the Wooden Man Form contains elements from all the empty hand forms and is a valuable tool in learning to flow effortlessly from technique to technique.

Advanced students have the opportunity to train with this "centre-piece" of the Wing Chun system, this is an opportunity afforded to very few schools as most work on an ad hoc basis, and their facilities do not allow the permanent stationing of this excellent training tool.

Muk Yan Jong is written in Chinese characters or in *han zi* as 木人樁; or in the *Chinese pinyin*: mù rén zhuāng, "wooden dummy")

The Muk Yan Jong form is performed against a "wooden dummy", a thick wooden post with three arms and a leg mounted on a slightly springy frame representing a stationary human opponent.

Although representative of a human opponent, the dummy is not a physical representation of a human, but an energetic and dynamic one.

Wooden dummy practice aims to refine a student's understanding of angles, positions, and footwork, and to develop full body power. It is here that the open hand forms are pieced together and understood as a whole.

At this point, I should mention something about 'living well'. This essentially means cutting out, or reducing your intake of, the following:-

- Smoking
- Alcohol
- Caffeine
- Sugar
- Foods high in carbohydrates

Equally you should look to increase your intake / uptake of:-

- Water (boil it and then chill it, then drink at room temperature)
- Vegetables and fruit (but don't get too hung up on this 'five a day' thing, it's a sense of balance you should strive for)
- Gentle exercise where-ever possible, for example walking, going up steps, standing on one leg (less funny than it sounds, you can practise this to improve balance)

Closing chapter notes: *A conditioned fighter who has honed his skills and can control his mind, and thus, how he re-acts to the various stresses of a fight situation, can be a very dangerous fighter indeed. Some might say that to master the physical aspects of your Art will not be enough—to master those elements where your emotions, and how you react during combat, are significant in how they affect the outcome. Master both elements, and you will be a formidable opponent indeed.*

5

Advanced Methodology

Don't be static or predictable as a fighter.
Be varied in attack and make yourself difficult to read.

Chapter focus: *This particular chapter is not necessarily aimed at beginners in martial arts, however it is still worthwhile that you read it if you are new to your particular style or Art.*

*   *   *

As you advance in your skills, *feel* your opponent's energy. You should be able to stop him before he has even gotten his attack off. Kill the monster while it is little.

*   *   *

Remember that if you allow your opponent to grow in confidence you hasten your defeat. Bruce Lee is quoted as saying 'I will beat any man in this room within sixty seconds'. With the greatest of respect to Bruce, that is about fifty seconds too long. End the fight quickly . . . take more than ten seconds to do it against most people, and you are doing something seriously wrong!

Of course Bruce was talking about martial artists of a decent standard so I would say, make it sixty seconds on the outside, but no more than that.

*   *   *

Think, for a moment, about the basic Wing Chun kick. It is *so low* with regard to the height at which it is applied that you can use a stop-kick against your opponent's attempt at kicking you. Such is the beautiful simplicity of the primary Wing Chun kick.

*   *   *

You should feel your opponent's energy. What this means is—until we grow an extra arm or leg, there are only so many attacks an opponent can do. Do not be concerned with this, as you are equal to him in this respect. Feel the opponent's energy, and use it to despatch him.

*   *   *

Be first. Be hardest. Be fastest. I've mentioned this before, and mention it here again because it applies, every single time. Certainly you can be first off with your attack, or even second, from a counter attacking point of view. Certainly my style as a fighter, as a counter-attacker, has always worked for me. But if I need to dominate from the start, throughout, and to the end result, I can do this, and it is what anyone who studies martial arts should strive to do.

*   *   *

The boldest attack often prevails. If you have the fullest of confidence in what you are doing, demonstrate it in your actions. Note that 'confidence' should be read as being confident in your ability based on your experience and your skill—not cockiness. There is no room for that in martial arts, and those that act in that way are often found out, and quickly.

*   *   *

The confident martial artist knows his strengths, but knows his weaknesses too. You can defeat your opponent with ease by understanding both aspects of yourself.

*   *   *

Do not let anyone shake your belief in who you are. It takes courage to face your own demons and be aware of your own shortcomings. You do not need anyone else to put you down. Only if they dare to meet you and prove themselves in combat can they say if their way is better than your own. Even if they were to beat you, it does not mean you have failed, just on the day, in that moment, they prevailed. Learn from it, and come back, and beat them on the return.

*   *   *

Always walk away from a fight situation if you can. The smart fighter will always do this.

*   *   *

If you find yourself in a situation where you cannot avoid fighting, then you must do everything to come through it as safe as you can. Your life, and your loved ones lives could depend on it.

*   *   *

Respect the laws of your country and adopt a high moral code. But do not become a statistic just because you were frightened of the consequences of using your skills. Everyone has the right to defend themselves.

*   *   *

Closing chapter notes: *Do not get involved in petty squabbles with faceless non-entities. You may be cut up by another driver, so let it go. So long as you are safe, what matter? Why get involved in a fight so needlessly? Be the bigger and better person, and rise above all that.*

This chapter is deliberately short. I could write many more things here, but there is no need. There are loads of things to learn and apply in your training from this chapter if you read it through thoroughly and apply the methods properly.

6

Re-directing your Opponents Energy

Or how to defeat him without even throwing a punch.

Chapter focus: *Despite what martial arts students or non-martial arts people may think, it is not always about aggressive techniques.*

In this chapter, consideration is given to how you can despatch an opponent without actually 'going in hard'.

Whilst it is fair to say that much of the chapter focus from the Arts point of view surrounds Tai Chi, do not think that this does not apply to you. The martial artist who learns to re-direct his opponent's energy can often do it with ease, if following some of the advice given in this chapter.

Could it be said that this really is the real way to fight, by not fighting at all?

You may have heard of Yin and Yang :

Yin*: Characterised by soft flowing movements, it is the gentle, soft, slow, graceful, feminine side of Tai Chi.*

Yang*: Characterised by hard, powerful movements, this is the strong, fast, fluid, masculine side of Tai Chi.*

If you try to meet force with force every time you face an attack, your attack has to be superior to your opponents. For example, if you leave your arms down or to the side when you place a front kick towards your opponent's stomach, if his block is better than your attack, yours will fail. If you are less committed than him, your attack will fail.

If two cars collide at 60 mph, the collision is at 120 mph and so the results of the opposing forces are twice as devastating.

And so, how to minimise the risk? For the foolish martial artist rushes in like a bull with no game plan, and no plan 'b' if things go wrong. You cannot always fight your way out of the situation when dealing with a superior opponent.

Tai Chi Chuan, Taijiquan or even 'Tai Chi' as it is more commonly known, has no obvious outward aggressive movements, at least, not initially. To the majority who see it, it doesn't really look like a martial art at all.

When the Western mind is brought up with boxing, street fighting, and UFC—you wonder what place Tai Chi could have as a fighting art. Indeed, to call it that is to cheapen it. Tai Chi Chuan is the ultimate martial art in many ways, as it is an art for health, spirituality, your mental well being, and physical conditioning.

Tai Chi is unique in this respect. I won't ever say or impress on someone, or try to influence them that one art is superior to all others, in my own personal view, it is the art one should try to excel at after you have tried so many other martial arts.

One can make a decision on what style to practise when he has all the available information.

One common misconception is that Tai Chi is too slow, too soft, to be of any practical use. One well meaning but less informed friend of mine even referred to Tai Chi as being 'for the fairies'. Well, you have to understand why you are doing Tai Chi—or if you *don't* understand, why *others* practise Tai Chi.

It could be any number of reasons, but these are the main reasons:

- Health
- Balance
- Control
- Good Posture
- Stronger body-bones, and internal organs
- Learn how to cultivate the 'vital air' or Qi Gong
- Learn an Art
- Learn forms and have a structure to the exercise routine
- Learn a martial art that does not have the punishing repetitive routines of other arts like Kung Fu, Karate, Tae Kwon Do etc.
- As a top-up to the seasoned martial artist. By 'top-up', I mean the 'top layer' of a martial artist's skill, prowess and expression

Tai Chi, in many ways, is the ultimate martial art. Why do I say this? Well, for one thing, it is an art that always keeps giving. To say you have mastered Tai Chi would be fraudulent. Oh yes, you can be a Tai Chi Master, but that in itself should not infer you are the master of Tai Chi. There's a difference. A big one. And it is this:-

It is one of those Arts that you never truly get perfect at. Rather, you are striving for perfection in it. In Karate and Kung Fu, you can have synchronised form practise, so *Bassai Dai* or *Chinto*, or *Siu Lim Tao* or *Biu Jee* forms will look largely the same, especially so if the students demonstrating the forms have the same teacher. With Tai Chi, the forms are sometimes so complex (and this is especially true of the Chen style).

Given what I have learned about the Art over the years, it is interesting that it is considered too slow to be effective. Tai Chi has often surprised me as a student, and as a teacher in just how really alarmingly effective it is.

For example, because Tai Chi helps you be rooted from the ground, and, if you are learning it properly, you will be built from the 'ground up'.

There are three primary components of Tai Chi and are:-

- **Forms**—where a series of movements are made in a set sequence and the pace is not slow, but actually performed at a measured pace
- **Tui Shou** (pronounced 'tway-show') or 'pushing hands'—the practice of Tui Shou often involves two practitioners and is sometimes thought of as 'the Kung Fu of Tai Chi' because there is an element of combat involved. Practitioners of Tui Shou often 'lock forearms' against each other and attempt to literally 'push' their opponent away. Tai Chi being an essential gentle art and form of moving meditation, the aim would not be to knock or push your opponent over. The objective is to feel the other person's energy and re-direct it, nothing more. Often they will reciprocate and you will have to know how and when to yield. Most important is to keep your balance which, if you have learnt the Forms well, you are more likely to keep your balance against someone who has not spent an appropriate amount of time on

Form work. As to how long one should practise these Forms, the correct answer would be 'as much as you can, and as often as you can.'

- **Qi Gong** (pronounced '*chee gun-g*'). Whilst they are separate, they are related, and more correctly, 'interlocked' with each other. If you just practise the Forms, your Tai Chi will be 'okay', but not where it could be, or where it needs to be. If you go up against someone who does understand Tai Chi from the martial, art, and the spiritual side of the style, you may find yourself beaten, and wondering just how it happened. Such is the power and effectiveness of Tai Chi Chuan.

In *Pushing Hands*, for example, you could get overwhelmed. I know I did, against Guo Sifu and Master Chen, and many of my students have when I've used it. It works, *alarmingly* well.

It is far better then, to end a fight, if it has to happen at all, with almost no aggressive attacks being thrown. The fighter who is tense will often, if not always lose. How many times have you heard someone say 'loosen up / chill out !'

The more relaxed you are, the more you are able to repel your opponents attack. Even if it is an extremely aggressive attack on you, *feel* that energy come at you, and re-direct it elsewhere.

Sounds easy, doesn't it? The reality is, many people 'revert to type' and may start to punch and kick out, forgetting the principles they may have experienced in class.

Tai Chi is the best martial art for redirecting the opponents energy, because it uses non-aggressive movements (and therefore you will be more relaxed executing them) the other styles such as Karate, Kung Fu and Jeet Kune Do can also achieve this 're-direction', but perhaps, to slightly lesser effect.

This is because often you are taught to 'fight force with force' and this is an improper use of the skills you are learning.

So whether or not you repel an opponents attack with force using say an 'external' art like Kung Fu, or an 'internal' art like Tai Chi—whatever happens, make sure it is effective. Otherwise, you will think that skill is no good whereas the truth is more likely to be you did not execute it properly.

That is why you got hit, when it should have been avoided!

*   *   *

The more advanced you are in your training, the more you have to hold back and show proper restraint. Kung Fu, Karate and Jeet Kune Do are often viewed as very aggressive martial arts, but surely the ultimate aim is to not fight at all?

Some of the best moves in martial arts are those where a opponent can be defeated by you, by not throwing a single punch. What does this mean in practise? Surely you must attack an opponent with everything you have, right?

Not necessarily. In fact, many of the techniques I have employed over the years are used to nullify an opponents attack.

Look at the primary blocks in Wing Chun Kung Fu, for example.

Wu Sao—your guarding arm. If you keep it in the centre of your chest, not too close, not too far away, it is always in the optimum position to stop an attack to the centre line.

Pak Sao—This is not literally a 'slapping block'. If you condition properly, a well placed pak sao is a deadly weapon that will re-direct your opponent's attack with ease.

You can also use it to 'deaden' someone's arm by simply extending it as the attack comes towards you.

Lap Sao—This wonderful technique literally pulls the attacking arm towards your direction, and then away from you. Timed right, you can floor an attacker by using lap sao applied right on the wrist (where the arm is often weakest—especially if you do not practise Wing Chun).

If you use the lap sao grab to the inside of the attacking arm, you can gently and successfully take the opponent to the ground, because when you apply it, his legs will begin to give way.

Some of the other techniques like *Tan Sao, Gan Sao, Gum Sao* and others are more invasive than those listed above. For that reason I am going to refer to them more in a book on *Kung Fu*, later.

Unorthodox moves could be where you punch an opponent's arm to give him, in effect, a 'dead' arm.

Closing chapter notes: *A move which flows, is more effective because it changes and adapts to the opponent's energy and movement. If you put your all into a move, only for it to fail, you will soon realise that flowing moves work better than static ones.*

Put this in practise and you will soon reap the benefits.

7

Self-Defence Principles for Women

Gender doesn't define the outcome of a fight. Skill, guile and smart thinking does.

Chapter focus: *Don't be fooled by the chapter title. This chapter should be read by male and female students, or those interested in learning some core self defence principles.*

The appropriate focus though, is predominantly on how women and girls deal with a potential threat to their lives, and are encouraged to utilise some of the techniques contained therein.

Women and young girls have often asked 'How can I deal with HIM? He's bigger, stronger, and more powerful than I am.'

It is true that men, in general, are physically more powerful than women. A woman cannot hope to beat a man who is bigger and stronger than her, hand to hand. But this should not infer that her situation is hopeless.

A different set of principles are needed then, to defeat such an adversary. Not only a different set of principles, but an understanding of body mechanics. Here, women can draw on the similarities between the two genders, and execute a plan of attack that works.

That doesn't mean women learn the system differently. But this is where a group format might just weaken the training. An instructor who knows the difference needs to draw out the strengths and minimise the weaknesses of the different students.

For women, they often are giving away a lot of weight, height and reach if they are fighting a man, and that is just for starters.

It can be very intimidating to fight someone much bigger than yourself. Even some men may admit to that, and prefer to fight someone their own height or perhaps smaller than themselves.

When I teach a female student, it is the same as teaching a male student in the sense that the system is the same, just the tactics may be altered to fit that certain individual.

If you don't believe that this can work, come and train with me. I'll show you how it works!! It is not fixed positions, that only 'this' is 'this' and' this' is 'that', it is something that works because it is based on reality, on what 'could' happen, in a given situation.

Here is the scenario: Put a man in front of a woman and tell them both they are about to engage in combat. The man will think 'I can easily beat this woman' and the woman thinks 'I'm going to get seriously hurt by this man.' If you were to change the dynamics in terms of how this situation could be thought of, instead of being predictable, a new theory, and set of possibilities emerge.

There are obvious differences in the physical stature of a man and a woman, but the body mechanics remain largely the same. Both sexes have two arms, two legs, a torso and a head. If you know where to attack on each weak point, then the 'smarter' opponent will prevail. It is not a 'done-deal' that the man will win every time.

I have trained women who were sufferers and victims of domestic violence. I don't like such terms being applied to these very brave women, because what they have gone through, I cannot begin to imagine. However, the fact they are there in class, and ready to train and learn from me (a male) says a lot about them, and the strong sense of character in them. A mere man should not be able to take that sense of 'self-worth' and 'self-esteem' from a woman, but many attempt to do just that.

In the classes I show women how they should approach a physical fight with a man. And I have been in a lot of classes where the techniques seemed great, but this is in the class. The issue I have with this is—the natural generated effect of true channelled aggression causes what is called an "adrenaline dump". This 'fear-induced' high volume shot of adrenaline is normal and natural, and cannot be stopped, even by experienced black belts or some experts in their chosen style.

The effects of this adrenaline dump can be utterly devastating, especially if you are not prepared for it.

The main problem is that many of the techniques that are taught in traditional women's self defence training are rather complex or too complicated for the average person to properly execute. Or maybe they can do it, but put them in a real scenario where they could be hurt, and what happens is, they freeze.

Unless you are a real expert in what you do . . . and it would be fair to say many that attend a self-defence class will not be—complex techniques may not be as well executed in the reality when compared to practise (and the relative safety of the training area), if at all, when the heat really is on and adrenaline levels are high.

Many of the martial arts / self-defence systems utilise joint locks and in some cases, pressure points that require years of training to properly execute. Do you have time to learn that, if you are say, a victim of domestic violence, or a woman who was subjected to extreme violence by someone you didn't know, like in a rape or mugging situation? Sometimes even when they are applied properly to someone who has an unusual amount of joint flexibility or a very high resistance to pain, they don't work.

I'm not knocking the values taught in systems like Aikido or Krav Maga, they have their merits, it is just that you do need to know your stuff. It is hard to learn that in just one or a handful of lessons, and you going away thinking 'this won't work!' The likelihood, after years of practise is that is will work, but you just need to know it, and in today's world, too few have time for that. It is a shame.

Knowing your 'space' and how to dominate it whilst using good verbal skills (i.e. screaming/shouting to make sure others around you will hear you are in trouble) means a high percentage of attacks can be avoided or diffused altogether. It certainly would make a potential assailant think twice.

Remember if you scream, a man will try and cup his hands over your mouth. The strength of your whole hand can break his finger, or bite through. You don't need to know years of martial arts training in order to be able to do this—but you do need to be able to go through with it. That does take some confidence.

Think about the alternative for a second if you are feeling a bit squeamish.

There's another problem in that a great number of the techniques taught were not designed especially for women. They require too much upper body strength which many women simply don't have.

Many of the martial arts teach kicking techniques that are great for the studio or for sport competition, but are all but useless on the street. Unfortunately many of you are led to believe that you can really use these kicks effectively in a combat situation. You will end up with a false security believing you can defend yourself with such techniques. In reality, if you ever have to really protect yourself, you can get yourself into trouble very quickly.

Many techniques require years of training or are just impossible to learn unless you are under the direct training of the master instructor. You cannot learn these properly from a video, book or seminar. They take years to perfect, even under the supervision of an expert instructor.

A lot of what is taught is just too fanciful! It doesn't stand a chance to work in a real attack!

Understanding weaknesses in the human body:-

To beat someone bigger than you, you have to understand where they are vulnerable. For a man, his primary weaknesses are these:-

The *groin*. If a man is kicked or receives a well placed knee in this area, he will be in considerable pain, to the point of passing out. The Wing Chun neutral basic stance allows some protection from this, in that you can drop your height, and in so doing protect your groin, but what if you don't know the stance, or how to 'drop' so as to protect yourself, you will be hit hard.

The *shin*. In Wing Chun Kung Fu particularly, the first basic kick or 'heel' kick is a leg technique which helps you to strike the opponents shin with speed and power. The beauty and simplicity of this kick is that anyone can do it, because it is not a high kick (so flexibility is not a factor). You just need to be able to strike hard, fast and low.

A woman who is wearing her high heel shoes for example, will be able to exert a huge amount of pain by striking the man's leg there. Note that you do not kick by pointing the toes (you will break them against the shin!) it is a 'heel' kick, meaning you strike by using the heel of your foot. It is a very simple, but very powerful, effective technique.

The neck. This area is protected by a rather thin layer of skin. It is also an area you can reach pretty easily, given that most men are taller than women, the neck is a primary area to go for.

How can you attack the neck? Well, as many women have long fingernails, if you use 'Wing Chun' you can use the closing 'Bon Sao' movement from the *Siu Lim Tao* form, or, more simply, scratch the neck on the one side, withdraw the arm and place a well-aimed chop to the neck on the other.

The eyes. If you hit one eye, even softly, both eyes will water and so he will be unable to see, and so, find it much more difficult to fight back. You can also throw things towards his eyes, like road dirt for example. It has a blinding, paralysing effect that, for a few moments at least, is hard to recover from. By that time, hopefully you would have had ample opportunity to make your escape.

Fingers. Your hand is stronger as a unit, than his one or two fingers. Therefore, if a man grabs at you, don't try and move his whole arm with your hand. It is unlikely you will be able to do it. But grab his finger—the little one is best—and the whole dynamic of the situation changes in an instant. And you have the upper hand, so to speak.

Hair. If you can grab or pull his hair, this will hurt—a lot. It may not always be possible, as many men shave their head, but it is but one option for you amongst many.

The stomach. This may be a surprise inclusion, but remember the stomach is a large area of the body, and largely, a soft area of the body, which makes it a good target. You are hardly likely to miss with a well placed front kick.

Jewellery. This works both ways. If he is wearing a ear-ring, yank at it and pull it off. Similarly, if you have jewellery you can use, such a necklace you can lash it at his face, throw a bangle or bracelet by directing it towards his eyes. Or you can spray perfume into his eyes. Whatever it is that keeps you safe, you are encouraged to do it.

Too often the primary reaction is to 'freeze', or even scream, but this will only irritate the man (or woman, even) and exacerbate the situation. The best thing to do, if you cannot run away from the situation, is to try one of the above.

However, that's the ideal opportunity to strike.

Let's look at the body as a whole. You can attack the back of the leg which will immediately destabilise his balance. This requires a simple push of your knee into the back of his leg. Again, if you understand 'stances' and how to shift body weight, you will be more effective at what you do.

Those who say it is about weight are wrong. It is all about body mechanics. If enough pressure is applied in the right area, and everyone has these weak areas, even martial arts teachers who have an air of invincibility about them are susceptible to this. Of course, such people tend to know about stances and shifting body weight, and how to properly distribute it in order to stay balanced and focused.

If you don't want to get that close, instead of using your knee, use the full extension of your leg. It does not matter how big or strong this person is, as humans, we are all weak from a kick to the back of the leg.

Focus on kicking higher up, and kick to the groin.

Scratch hard into the neck or face. Push your fingers towards his eyes, if you have to. It isn't complicated, and it does work. Have confidence in it and yourself.

One thing to note is, you must not be half-hearted about an attack. If you hesitate, even for a moment, you allow that person the chance to come back into the fight, and really, the aim should be to finish the fight as soon as possible.

The law: Of course there are laws about what you can and cannot do. My view is that everyone has the right to defend themselves. What the law considers a 'reasonable level of force' varies from country to country and also regionally. There does not seem to be a standard set of rules that apply, and the punishment that is dealt out by courts often does not fit the crime.

One hopes this will change, because even police groups that I have taught, express frustration that the real culprits are not punished.

Closing chapter notes: *There is nothing more sickening in my view than a man who attacks a woman. There are too many stories about a woman getting raped, or even killed. In nearly all these cases a man is doing the attacks and the penalties are never severe enough.*

I believe strongly that women who learn good self-defence techniques become confident women in their dealings with such male aggressors. In the end these 'men' can be found out as being what they are—cowards.

Every woman has a right to defend herself and I hope some of the techniques in this chapter help to cement that view and ability.

8

Groups & 1-2-1 Training

Chapter focus: *I have taught groups, schools, and personal training for years. Both methods of training have their merits. I want to explain to you each way that I teach them, the advantages and disadvantages of each.*

In a formal class structure, students will be expected to address the instructor with his or her given title.

Karate: The correct title is *Sensei (pronounced Sen-Say)*

Tai Chi / Kung Fu: The correct title to use is Sifu (pronounced 'Shif-foo'—Mandarin / pronounced 'See-Foo'—Cantonese).

Let us look at the one-to-one side of teaching and learning, first.

People often think personal training is expensive. I would say such a method is not exactly the cheapest way to train, but you need to understand the type of student that would undertake this style of training, but also find a teacher willing to impart knowledge perhaps more quickly than you would get in a group format. Usually such a student comprises these attributes:-

Highly committed: Such a student will work with the instructor but also listen to him so that mutual but achievable goals are set. Sometimes I have been asked these questions, to which I provided these answers:-

"Can I train two, three or five times a week with you?"

Of course they can, if I'm available to teach them. Their standard, provided there is a sufficient rest period between intensive lesson, will get very good and develop a real quality over time. The instructor has to also consider the student's motives for training regularly.

Forget about money for a moment. A martial arts teacher of true worth is more passionate about his teaching rather than the income it generates, although of course that is important as a re-investment in the School.

Similarly, a student that is passionate about martial arts has to decide how good he wants to get, and how best to go about it.

The starting point for such a student can be asked by this question:-

Where am I now? (in respect of my training, ability and goals)

The question is very open ended though. You may feel you have instantly improved by merely watching a Kung Fu movie. The reality is, you will know that where-ever you currently are in your training, that watching movies alone cannot improve your actual real skill.

That is something that only comes with very hard practise.

Where do I want to be?

Before a student begins martial arts training, there are certain reasons for doing so. It could to build more confidence, to get fitter, or—to achieve a high standard in the Art. Attaining a black belt or black sash for example.

How do I get there?

This is a most critical question. To do so in the correct manner, a prospective student will seek out a teacher who can take the student where he wishes to go. At the very least, the good instructor will set out the path on which the student should follow.

Choose poorly, however, for example the 'Twelve Months to Black Belt' programs you see advertised in the martial arts media, and you will lose out far more than you expect to gain.

It follows the adage that 'nothing worthwhile is ever easy'.

It is especially important in today's various distractions that the 'something worthwhile' is hunted down. Time is so precious we have to spend it wisely. You can save money, but not time, so find that good teacher, with a progressive syllabus, to teach you a system that works—a system for 'life'.

Which way is best?

You can train on your own, or with a video you see on-line, and perhaps you can kid yourself that you are learning. Most 'video tuition' is by its very nature a 'passive' form of education and in the end, could only really serve as a guide, but no more than that.

The best way is to find a good teacher, as aforementioned. Ultimately if the teacher you have is just not working for you, don't feel some sense of obligation. You are the one paying your money, and investing your time.

I should also mention the value of books as this particular one concerns itself with martial arts.

You can learn a lot from a book, even martial arts books. But I think you really have to read, re-read, to try comprehend what is being discussed, practise it hard as per your understanding, and even discuss with a martial arts teacher the specific points raised in the book. If he says 'that is nonsense' then ask him in his opinion, why that is so.

How do I make sure that I achieve my goals?

Be prepared mentally. Understand what you are undertaking, or at least attempt to do so.

Be prepared physically. Martial arts training is not for the faint of heart. It is difficult, which is as it should be.

Be prepared mentally. Expect knocks, feelings of stagnation, a lack of progress. Don't let it bother you. Stay true to your course and be very single minded and determined. Whilst you are doing all this, imagine what you are actually achieving along the way.

A teacher's right to refuse to teach someone. If a student wants a quick fix way to learn and bash the hell out of someone, it is best you don't teach them, and I certainly would not teach them if they showed such attributes. Sometimes they won't even have to tell you. As a teacher, you get to identify this quite easily over time, which could be within seconds in some cases.

"Where should I be after five years if I train with you twice a week?"

Hopefully you will have progressed to a decent standard in the system. No one student is the same, and it is here where the personal one to one training comes into its own.

Training twice a week means the student will be indoctrinated into the syllabus in more depth, more quickly. It might be too much to absorb. It certainly does not mean you will skip parts of the program, you will do it as exactly the same way as the other students. There is a set standard, it is that what has to be achieved. So after five years, you might just be on the later stages of the system, or slightly ahead, or slightly behind. As an instructor I have always pushed students hard to make up as much of the syllabus as they can.

Wanting to achieve something in their life: The student will understand and accept that they will not get a black belt in 12 months, no matter how hard or how regular they train. Whatever belt they get, they will have earned it. Anyone who promises you an early black belt is not someone you should associate yourself with.

Ask yourself honestly, if you were handed a black belt within twelve months, could you really deal with someone who earned his or her black belt over a 5 to 7 year period? What I am saying is, if it is easy, *too easy*, it is not worth it. You would be best off going and buying a belt coloured black, just so you can convince yourself, but you won't be able to convince anyone else. Sorry, but this is how it is.

Focused, determined: As a student, you will understand and accept that whilst your skills will improve, the difficulty of each new grade attained will also be a factor on how badly you want to be, the person you want to be. As you progress, you must retain the knowledge of previous syllabuses, and also maintain that standard set.

To lose your focus, or in other words, to only be thinking of a black sash or belt . . . well, you are not really paying attention to the belt you are currently on. The focused student knows to only focus on that syllabus alone, and remains determined enough to see it through to the next level. That is the sort of student you should aim to be.

Refuse to let anything else get in the way of their lesson: Modern life is busy, and everyone knows how many distractions there are out there. Sometimes it is completely unavoidable, like work or family issues, but what sets high achieving students—those who stick doggedly to the system and make it to lessons, or make them up if they are missed, apart from those who always have an angle to get out of it are the sort of students that impress me.

I have never wanted a black belt academy. I much prefer a smaller set of students who value the training and instruction I give them and carry it in their every action. Not in a show-off way of course, but in a way that shows they have learned great self-discipline, confidence, and respect for others.

What about group training then?

Groups are great for training with people of your own level, and often just above or below your level. Also, there is a great social aspect to it and people thrive on the atmosphere of the class.

Depending on the instructor's teaching style, many may find the lessons somewhat less intense than personal tuition. If you take it that in a group lesson the instructor will not be 'on your case' the whole time, and you are fine with that, you may enjoy this style of teaching.

It is understandable. Often, as a young student, when an instructor I really respected passed by me, I would instantly try and do better, only to do the technique worse, more often than not.

I suspect this has happened to many students too, but the important thing is to carry on like nothing happened—*that is your external defence*, but internally, you should make sure you do your best to make things right from that point forward. Because, you can bet the instructor will pass your way again.

That is what an instructor does in a lesson. If the group is comprised of thirty or more students say, can you really expect the instructor to devote loads of attention to specific students? He or she does not have the time. But, we do our best . . . if you are a new student, or recently graded, a good instructor will take the time to explain and demonstrate the new techniques to you.

You will hopefully then make a concerted effort to really do the techniques well, and the instructor will be back, one would hope, in a few moments rather than when half the lesson had passed.

An instructor may repeat lesson techniques over and over again that same week. So let us say you missed one lesson the previous week—you did two lessons when you usually do three, but in this coming week you pay for five lessons.

Four of those five lessons turn out to be basically the same, albeit with a few different students you don't normally see because you don't go on those nights as a rule.

So . . . was it a waste? Of your time, no, because any physical activity is good and especially training related to martial arts. You may have found your money was wasted though . . . one look at the syllabus would tell you that you could have practised some of those movements at home.

But of course if you don't go regularly, the instructor doesn't notice you. And what if there is more than one instructor at the club? You get a different type of lesson, sure, but that may be where the benefit ends.

Of course most students train via the group method and, for all of its flaws, it is still a solid foundation with which to progress to the senior levels.

For those wanting to scale to greater heights though, you should seek out a instructor who can take you to that level. Do not take the word of the first instructor you meet, try and find more than one so you have a point of reference to compare them too. Because, once you choose an instructor, you have to get used to his or her way of teaching.

Closing chapter notes: *Both one-to-one personal training and group classes have their advantages and disadvantages. You need to decide which is right for you. I would suggest (if money allows) that 1-2-1 personal training is the way to go every time, provided you find an instructor who will push you and that you will feel the benefit in every lesson.*

There are still those who will enjoy the group format and it has many benefits. Decide whether you want the long haul but gentle or the slightly faster journey but far more intensive, and go from there.

9
Tai Chi

The Supreme Ultimate Art.

Chapter focus: *The title of this subject, Tai Chi, offers insights into this most ancient of martial arts. This is an Art which deserves a book just for itself, because the intricacies of it are so varied.*

The forms are many and varied, and include basic open hand forms but also weapons forms. I do not need to go into detail on those specific forms here, but you will get a general appreciation from the chapter to know where you need to start.

It is very difficult for me to come up with enough superlatives about Tai Chi. To give it the name the Chinese call it, *Taijiquan,* it roughly translates as the supreme or great ultimate fist.

But before I tell you what it is, I should really tell you what it is not, because there are many views about what Tai Chi actually is, and most of these I have found to be incorrect.

It is not:

A soft Art: For those who do kick boxing or are into UFC—The Ultimate Fighter Championship, they look on Tai Chi as something that looks like some form of dance or ballet. It certainly does not look like a martial art, for the most part anyway.

Just for old people: You know, anyone can do Tai Chi, young / old, male / female . . . it really doesn't matter. Just because older people tend to practise Tai Chi, it does not mean that they alone practise Tai Chi. I myself did not start as early as I should have done.

If you ask someone what Tai Chi is, can you really expect them to know? To some, it's 'the one with the slow, graceful movements, like a dance . . .' to others 'isn't that the one old people do?'. Others still may say, 'I don't know what it is, just looks like people shuffling about.'

Tai Chi, or Taijiquan to give it its proper name, translates as the 'supreme ultimate fist'. Does it sound so gentle now, or an art exclusively for the older generation?

Not a bit of it. When I was introduced to Tai Chi, I was already a black belt in Karate, and a black sash in Kung Fu. I thought myself an accomplished fighter. I didn't think that Tai Chi would have much to offer me. I expect I am not alone in that view, although, like most things, if you have a 'closed mind', you will limit yourself in so many ways.

What would an Art that seems initially no more than a slow ballet (and much less physical) have to offer? The movements seem not 'martial' at all and for this reason alone would be enough to keep martial arts enthusiasts away in their droves. In today's world, which is very much about doing things immediately and getting everything now, there are few people that would have the patience to learn an Art that doesn't offer a clear way to protect yourself, or, where needed, turn you into an effective fighter.

So what is the attraction of Tai Chi? Kung Fu has millions of followers the world over, with the Wing Chun estimated at around two million students.

Jeet Kune Do is less widely taught but there is huge interest in it, being the style that Bruce Lee bequeathed to the world.

Karate is the style steeped in Japanese tradition, and like the two former arts places a strong emphasis on fighting and good self defence.

My initial thoughts were this, that Tai Chi 'looks nice, gentle and . . . that's it'.

My introductions to it were in China, where I met one of my teacher's senior students. She had won major tournaments in China demonstrating her Tai Chi, and although I admit I had little idea of what she what really doing, it looked good. The presentation and execution was faultless.

From my experience, you cannot 'buy' a teacher's services in China in the way that is expected in Western countries. They either want to teach you, or they do not teach you anything. My first teacher never actually charged me anything although as I have mentioned, 'the payment' itself was related to what I was prepared to do as part of her training.

The origins of Tai Chi are such that even back then, it was steeped in secrecy. There are five main 'houses' of Tai Chi, which are Chen, Yang, Wu, Sun and Hao.

Most widely practised are Chen and Yang style, with Yang style very popular and is probably the most widely practised of all the styles. I could write a whole book, and series of books on Tai Chi itself so I will not do that here.

Chen style is the original Tai Chi style, and as such was meant to be the definitive Tai Chi. Yang came about when a man called Yang Lu Ch'an stayed at the Chen family home. He woke one night to see the Chen family practising some strange movements in the yard.

He had no idea what it was but was intrigued. Yang would watch the family practise every night and started to learn the movements himself. He was getting to a rather good standard himself when he was caught in the act by one of the Chen family. Two of the brothers set upon him in order to teach Yang a lesson, but he had learned the movements so well, and added modifications of his own, that he defeated the two brothers with relative ease.

After that, there was no learning in secret. The Chen family invited Yang to learn from them, and he showed them some of his style. It evolved over the years of course, but it was in effect, his own version of Tai Chi and it is that style, the Yang style that is the most widely practised today.

I will talk more about Yang Lu Ch'an in a future text as he is a very interesting character, as you would expect any founder of a 'good' style to be. He became a bit of a legend in his own right, as he has a style which could defeat opponents and yet not seriously injure them. Some would say this is the attainment of the most supreme level achieved in martial arts.

Miss Zhu Zi, Master Guo's student, trained with me. I suspected she was sent to me so that Master Guo and Master Zhao (his teacher in Chen style Tai Chi) could see if I was up for it.

I tried some basic strikes to get a feel for her blocking and intercepting technique and she was adept at evading, such was the excellence of her positioning. That said, we were only trying from a standing position but by using Tui Shou, the art of 'pushing hands' (which is kind of like the 'Kung Fu' of Tai Chi), she became virtually impossible to shove around.

That is why Tai Chi perhaps is the ultimate martial art. You do everything from a relaxed position and if you are relaxed, in body, mind and spirit, your whole being will react when it needs to.

That is not to say you would do a Tai Chi application in the same speed as you would do the form. Of course not. The primary benefit of performing the routines is health.

But if you need to move with speed in order to counter an attack, then it must be done from a relaxed position, but in no way a slow one. However, because you would learn Tai Chi correctly, you will have more time than you think (certainly more than your opponent would think) in order to be proactive in your counter attack.

To be more precise in Tai Chi, read counter attack as a *counter defence*, because Tai Chi is never aggressive, yet you can learn to deal with aggressors with ease.

That is the highest level you could attain in martial arts, where you do not have to attack an opponent in order to defeat him.

Closing chapter notes: *There are many Schools teaching Tai Chi out there, and in my experience only Yang and Chen styles are worth bothering with.*

Yes, the 42 Step form has Sun and Wu style Tai Chi in it, but the main parts are from Yang and Chen. For the amount of time and effort required to learn this Art, I advise you to go for Chen or Yang. In my view, the other styles are not good enough to be of practical use. For you to benefit from this 'supreme martial art', choose the style that works for you—in class and in real life.

10

Kung Fu

Blow your opponent away, and don't place style over substance.

Chapter focus: *I am often asked by students the question 'Which is your favourite martial art?' and while I would certainly have a leaning towards Kung Fu, it just so happens I teach it the most, so have a closer affinity with it not only as a teacher but as a student.*

I do not expand in this chapter on the various styles of Kung Fu, for example Lau Gar, Hung Gar, Choy Li Fut, and others. This will be left for a future book that focuses solely on Kung Fu.

As well as giving a background to the story of Wing Chun, I open the chapter talking about my interest in Kung Fu, before going into more detail on the specific forms contained in the Wing Chun style that I predominantly teach.

I have always been interested in Kung Fu, even before I really knew what it was and how it differed from other styles of fighting. At first, I just wanted to concentrate on Karate because that is what I first trained in.

I was aware though, the club was teaching Kung Fu (also Judo)—so I decided if I could make enough progress on Karate, I would see about starting learning Kung Fu.

At first, it is too easy to say is Kung Fu is Chinese Karate, or that Karate is Japanese Kung Fu. They are both very different forms of self-defence.

I cannot be alone in my frustration when some parent may say 'my child is off to Karate practise now' when it is actually Kung Fu they are coming to, or vice-versa!

I would go as far as to say that Kung Fu is a very effective form of fighting, perhaps, having considered some others in some depth over the years. Kung Fu, and specifically the style of Wing Chun, is the most effective form of fighting I have ever encountered.

That said, (unless it is one I have arranged), it won't serve you well in most tournaments. As most of the system—about 70% of it is illegal to use in tournaments, you are best sticking to a form of Karate or kick boxing for the trophy rounds. You can use Wing Chun, but you are limited in what you can use. That is for tournament rules of course. On the street, it's a different story, where you should use the right tool for the job.

Below: Picture taken in 1991, My first instructor in Kung Fu and Karate . . . Sifu Karen Li.

I make no exception to the rule that a martial art is primarily for self-defence, or for yourself and / or others who are in danger. You cannot, nor should not use the training—particularly of Wing Chun style Kung Fu, to seriously injure—or kill someone, where more restrained applications would be appropriate. There are laws that govern where you live and you cannot simply become a vigilante just because you have some martial arts training behind you.

So what is 'Kung Fu', exactly? The Chinese spelling in *pinyin* is *gongfu,* in which the literal translation is 'to work hard'. This should give anyone the clearest of statements in that to train in Kung Fu requires extreme dedication. You won't 'get' it overnight. It is a difficult system to master.

However, the Wing Chun style essentially strips out all the rubbish and nonsense usually associated with the 'flashy' (and largely ineffective) martial arts styles.

It is a system anyone, and by that I do mean, anyone, can learn. It is true that the style was originally developed by a woman, a Chinese nun by the name of Ng Mui. It wasn't called Wing Chun at that time.

The actual style Ng Mui used was called the 'plum fist flower' style. While it had a lot in common with the style that was to become Wing Chun, the creator of that style, Yim Wing Chun herself, thought the 'plum fist' style was more befitting for a man, than a woman, and so modified it to fit.

The story goes that Yim Wing Chun was being harassed by a out-of-town ganglord who wanted to marry her. She could not be less interested in him, but he became more threatening with each confrontation.
Yim Wing Chun was a strong minded girl, but this was a bit more than she could take. One day, Ng Mui found the girl crying on the roadside and, taking pity on her, inquired as to what was wrong.

Yim Wing Chun told Ng Mui the story of the bad ganglord and how she didn't want anything to do with him. She felt at the end of her tether though, and did not want to run away from her home province, but wondered what else she could do.

Ng Mui said she would be waiting the next time he turned, and sure enough, a week later he came to threaten Yim Wing Chun once again.

Standing beside her this time was Ng Mui, who told the ganglord to come back, not next week, but in six months time. She said to him 'If you can beat her in a fight, you can take her'.

He laughed at this, looking at the young girl with almost sneering disgust.

He vowed to beat her up on his return, and Ng Mui too, for having the temerity to keep him waiting.

Ng Mui looked rather pleased with herself but Yim Wing Chun looked terrified and asked the nun 'What do I do now? What have you gotten me into? I'm finished now!'.

Ng Mui explained that everything would be fine, that she was going to teach her how to defend herself. She told Yim Wing Chun that not only would she be okay, but that the ganglord would learn a very hard lesson indeed.

She mused 'Perhaps he won't be in any kind of state to chase after girls again, after you've finished with him!'

During the six months Ng Mui taught Yim Wing Chun her style of Kung Fu. Yim picked up the main elements quickly, and Ng Mui was pleased to see the hand speed and power the girl was harnessing.

After six months, the ganglord returned. He boldly stated 'I'm here to claim you, Yim Wing Chun ! No more delays now. Get out here, and bring that interfering nun with you'.

Ng Mui had prepared Yim Wing Chun for this day. Yim was quite prepared to go out and face him on her own, and so Ng Mui watched from indoors.

Yim walked straight up to her nemesis. She hadn't felt so brave and confident in any previous encounter. The ganglord went to grab her but he played literally into Yim's hands.

The fight, such as it was, was over in a matter of seconds. Yim had broken the man's arm, and several of his ribs. He left her alone and never visited her province again.

You would be forgiven then for thinking that Wing Chun is a 'soft' version of the many harder forms of Kung Fu. Not a bit of it.

Wing Chun adopts a 'centre-line' approach to both offensive and defensive movements. It is true to say that while it has many useful attacking techniques, it has no stand-alone blocking techniques. All blocking techniques, such as they are, are intended to become attacking movements. In most cases, you will even use the opponent as a lead-in to hit him.

There are some martial arts that won't offer you that. Of course, you have to be supremely confident in your ability to hit your opponent. Years of Wing Chun training offer a shortest possible distance to deal with your opponent. No fancy positions, postures, kicks or punches. You make contact with the opponent, break his guard, hit him, and return to a suitable defensive (or offensive) position.

What is meant by centre-line theory?

In theory, you will draw a vertical line on a person from head to toe. This means to attack the centre of the person by striking towards these areas. The focus is on these areas because if the attack is successful, the person is going to be beaten, and quickly so.

- Forehead
- Eyes
- Nose
- Mouth
- Chin
- Neck
- Upper part of chest

- Solar plexus
- Stomach
- Groin

Too much emphasis is often placed on style. Put simply, if you find the right style for you, and it works, what are you worrying about?

So many students (not the ones I continue to teach, I am happy to say) have said to me 'oh. I know Praying Mantis Kung Fu' or 'I did White Crane for a while'.

This isn't really important. What is important is what you do with the style you are devoting yourself to.

I'll be honest and say that I really do not wish to teach students who are obsessed with style over substance. Of course, it is fine to seek out new styles if you are not happy with the one you are doing, but if it is 'style for style's sake' then you are doomed to failure. Best not to mention you do it at all.

Now you are reading this and thinking 'Hang on, he is saying do not be concerned with styles and yet he is someone who has done Jeet Kune Do, Karate, Kung Fu, and two forms of Tai Chi. Surely that is hypocritical, no?'

No. Because these are the styles I have practised the most over the years. Yes, I have also practised Muay Thai Kick Boxing, Tae Kwon Do and some other styles.

But, so what? I find the styles I touch on most on this book are the ones that work for me. It may be different for everyone else, but sometimes you just find the right style for you.

As far as Wing Chun Kung Fu is concerned, by 1997, I had learned the entire system. That is not to say others could do it in the same amount of time. But I was dedicated, very focused, and between 1991-1996, was under the instruction of my great teacher Karen Li.

She taught me four primary forms, Siu Lim Tao, Chum Kiu. Biu Jee, and also a non—Wing Chun form called San Dan Chang Quan.

The three open hand forms are these:-

- Siu Lim Tao
- Chum Kiu
- Biu Jee

Siu Lim Tao translates as "way of the little idea" or "little idea form."

This form is the very essence of Wing Chun. It contains vital elements essential to energy and position training. Siu Lim Tao is the foundation of the Wing Chun system; all techniques flow from the basic movements of this form. As with all forms in the Wing Chun system, no techniques are superfluous; each has a practical application.

The importance and benefits of Siu Lim Tao cannot be overstated. Siu Lim Tao is not a one-time form—it is not learnt and then forgotten, just because it is the basic form. The student will obviously move on to better forms and more advanced techniques.

The teacher needs to emphasis that this form is practised constantly throughout a student's training, and hopefully, beyond.

Chum Kiu translates as searching or seeking the bridge; for example, likened to a bridging contact between two people.

Wing Chun is essentially a close quarter fighting art, and this form will enable students to master "closing in and closing down" on an opponent with correct positioning.

Whereas Siu Lim Tao is practised in a single stance, Chum Kiu introduces footwork and turning, both essential parts of the system. It is also the first time actual kicks are added to one's Wing Chun practise as far as the forms are concerned.

Biu Jee translates as the "thrusting (or striking) fingers" form. Its purpose is to refine energies and strikes and to recover from over-committed techniques. It is also known as the "first aid" form for this reason.

Biu Jee also contains some of the most devastating weapons in the Wing Chun canon, such as the finger-strike to the eyes and other weak points and elbow strikes.

For this reason, the student has to have mastered Siu Lim Tao and Chum Kiu before proceeding on to these extremely dangerous techniques. Once the student has (over a period of years) practiced all three forms, he or she will discover that they are complete in themselves.

My first teacher was instrumental in me learning these forms well. If not for her, I doubt I would have learned the entire system so well, or indeed add refinements to my own Kung Fu system so that Wing Chun itself was the bedrock, the foundation of a very demanding Kung Fu syllabus.

My Wing Chun syllabus is based on my original Sifu's system (Miss Li) although has some modifications. But all teachers have their own systems. Ultimately, there is a core that runs through Wing Chun that should mean that anyone who sees you demonstrate Siu Lim Tao, the first basic form, will know what it is that you are doing.

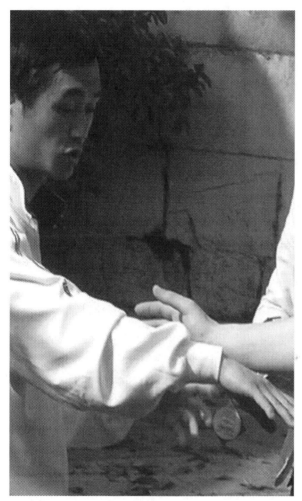

Left: Master Guo, my teacher in China)

It is not pure Wing Chun, but the majority of it is. It comprises elements of some other systems, including Ba Gua, Xing Yi, Shaolin, and Jeet Kune Do.

It is because of these refinements and inclusions that I believe my system would stand up with any other system in the world.

I teach students what I know. I have heard that some teachers hold back, thinking (rather arrogantly in my opinion) that the student is either not ready to learn or not worthy of the 'honour' of learning this 'secret society stuff' from the instructor.

This—is nonsense. You are either ready or you are not. The teacher will either share with you what he knows—once you have the maturity to understand it and deal with it. Or, he won't share the knowledge. That could be down to the concern that the student would use this knowledge in anger, in which case the teacher should have done more consultative groundwork to see if this person 'is that kind of student'. If so, why teach such a person?

I will accept that you can teach some people and they may be your student for a while, only to use these techniques in anger. Such is life—you cannot control another person's actions, or be held responsible for that. It happens.

However, you can minimise such things happening. If in a group format the same student causes problems again and again, then the instructor should take action. As a student, how many lessons have you been to where a particular student wants to take his bad day or general bad attitude out on someone who is just trying to learn good techniques and self-defence? Does this sound familiar to you?

In many respects Wing Chun is the ultimate fighting art, caring little for niceties, fancy moves, or flashy effects. It gets the job done quickly and efficiently and whilst there are many pretenders to its throne, you have to ask why a system like this that has been around for so long is still *the* one to learn?

True. The system has its flaws but it is one of the most 'flaw-less' systems out there. That's why there are over two million of Ip Man's (the master of Bruce Lee) descendants training in the world today. It is something about the brilliance of Wing Chun that the real figure of students training in the system may be closer to four million.

Closing chapter notes: *If a student wants to learn an effective way to fight, look no further than Wing Chun. It has three basic open hand forms, and preliminary techniques are easy to pick up.*

Similarly, if a student wants something easy to start with but hard to master, Wing Chun has it all.

I can think of no higher compliment to a fighting art that 'does exactly what it is supposed to' to say that anyone and everyone should have some knowledge of this very fine Art.

11

Karate

This style is not about fighting, but is more like finding a way to harmony. Find the secret to this, and you find balance in your life.

Chapter focus: *Karate is one of the best martial arts for giving a student discipline. Not just in the Art itself, but in life, For some, it might be too much. It was the first Art I learned, and as you will read, it gave me the balance I needed at a critical time in my life.*

As in the Tai Chi chapter, there are too many forms and styles to go into detail here. So what is appropriate is focus on the merits of Karate and the individual styles that I learned.

Karate was the first martial art I began to practise. I had just turned twelve years of age, and was in need of some fitness program I could actually enjoy, whilst at the same time having a most wonderful benefit of assisting me in protecting myself.

I was in a difficult period in my teens, and found adjusting to senior school rather difficult. I think some of the other children certainly contributed to this, but I found the support group, i.e. the teachers rather unsupportive and seemingly powerless to stop the constant fights I found myself in.

It is also true to say that I never enjoyed fighting but it became a 'must-learn' skill. I bemoaned the fact we had plenty of lessons on things I felt at the time were not really going to assist in my life later on. What I wanted, and needed, was something that was going to change my life, and for the better.

I had no idea where to start, although I knew of certain martial arts clubs in the city centre where I could train. The issue was, and remains a big issue for some of the students that come to train with me, is that group lessons can be intimidating. You don't know anyone, there are all different levels attending the same classes, and crucially, it takes longer to learn the skills in this format.

So the thing I needed most at that time, confidence—was not there, and I was a long way from getting it.

On approaching such clubs, and I did look at several, the same things that I did not like kept popping up again and again.

The buildings would look rather foreboding, and often the posters outside would show aggressive things, like a fist protruding from the clubs' logo and also pictures of the 'master' doing improbable looking techniques, such as flying through air and delivering a well placed side kick.

Even looking through the window you might see someone being thrown across the floor. And then, there is the shouting. Lots of it. And it can be very intimidating.

So although I was uncertain I was ready, I had already made the decision that I wanted to do some sort of formal training.

After a lot of research, I found Sifu Li's training centre, and the rest really is history.

* * *

A common misconception of the origins of Karate is that it came from Japan. If you mean the 'name' Karate, then that actually is true, but the styles inception was on the island of Okinawa.

Japanese invaders took on the local villagers. The feared Samurai, whether on horseback or not, sensed an easy victory against these peasant farmers. What they didn't know was, the Okinawans had developed their own particular 'warrior art', and because the main Art itself had no obvious weapons (unlike the Japanese Samurai with their swords, spears and other weaponry) to a degree the Okinawans could wait until an attack advanced on them, and then defeat the heavily armoured Japanese army.

If on horseback, the Samurai would be taken down by a flying side-kick to the chest, and most likely will have suffered serious internal injuries. The fall to the ground would be the least of the Samurai's worries. If the Okinawan followed up the technique, it would perhaps be to deploy a knife hand thrust to the chest or neck. Whatever he chose, the result would normally be death for the one on the receiving end.

It says a lot for this style that a villager could defeat one who has been trained to fight in an army. The style was called 'Okinawa-te' (te pronounced 'tay') and the Japanese soon learned to understand all about this Art, and called it 'kara-te', which means 'open' or 'empty' hand. In essence, no weapons are used, but when you progress through the *kyu* or students grades and then onto the *dan* grades you will be introduced to the weapons forms or, as they are known Japanese Karate, the '*katas*'.

Kata

Kata are very important in Karate. In fact, it could be argued that one who practises Karate, a 'Karate-ka' could be said to be excellent at Karate if he or she works hard at the katas. The reason is that all the techniques you would use in Karate, and the sparring principles too, have their foundation in kata practise.

However, a slight criticism of kata is that it does not have a true way to define and execute actions from the forms in sparring or real fighting.

It is an art sometimes considered by other martial artists as more like a sport or suitable only for tournament fighting. Perhaps it is more suitable because most of the techniques learnt can be used in a tournament and look good in that respect.

There are several moves in Karate that differ from Wing Chun, which was one reason I started training in Kung Fu. In Karate the emphasis is on power and body-twist.

At my School, we teach the Shotokan and Wado Ryu styles of Karate. Both are excellent styles that like all great martial arts styles, they actively promote discipline, well being, fitness, confidence and respect.

Karate (空手), Karate-dō (空手道), or Karate-do is a very popular martial art that developed from a group of indigenous Ryukyukuan fighting methods and Chinese kempo. "Karate" originally meant Te, or hand, or *open hand*, which was later changed to meaning *empty hand* in Japanese.

It is known primarily as a striking art, featuring punching, kicking, knee/elbow strikes and open handed techniques. However, grappling, joint manipulations, locks, restraints/traps, throws and vital point striking also appear in Karate. A student of Karate is called a Karate-ka which is written as 空手家.

In general, there are many components to modern Karate training. One common division is between the areas of:-

- **Kihon** (basics or fundamentals)
- **Kata** (the forms)
- **Kumite** (sparring)

Another popular division is between art, sport, and self-defence training.

It is perhaps unfortunate that in some martial arts circles that Karate is seen more as for tournament fighting than real street fighting.

Weapons (kobudo) comprise another important training area, as well as the psychological elements incorporated into a proper kokoro (attitude) such as perseverance, fearlessness, virtue, and leadership skills. Often in the execution of a technique, Karateka are encouraged to issue a loud kiai or 'spirit shout'.

Kata (Forms)

Kata—in Japanese script—型:かた—translates as a *form* or *set sequence of moves* and despite how they might appear to the outsider, they are not simply aerobic or cardio inducing routines.

They exist to demonstrate real, physical combat principles.
They were put in these sequences so that large and complicated movements could actually be recalled by invoking the name of the Kata or form.

There are many ways in which to interpret the forms for practical use, but in effect, if it is not useful, it should not be in the form.

There is a uniform way of doing these forms and katas, but expect variation between teacher, system, school and style. That is why a student should only rely on what his teacher instructs, because videos you can find on-line, or in other media, cannot be relied upon as being the best way to do the actual form. All it is, is different, and not necessarily better.

Basic forms in Karate (Wado Ryu style) are called the Pinan Katas and comprise:-

- Pinan Nidan
- Pinan Shodan
- Pinan Sandan
- Pinan Yondan
- Pinan Godan

These all comprise blocks and strikes, punches, kicks and jumps of increasing difficulty. They are designed to give a Karate-ka a set sequence of moves to deploy against an imaginary opponent, as well as enhancing stamina, skill and fitness.

Kumite (Sparring)

Kumite, or in the Japanese characters 組手:くみて) literally means "the meeting (or connection) of hands,".

Sparring may be constrained by many rules or it may be free sparring, and today is practiced both as sport and for self-defence training. Sport Karate sparring tends to be deployed as one hit "tag" type fights, purely for points.

Depending on the style or the teacher involved, takedowns and grappling may be involved alongside the punching and kicking.

Types of Kumite

- Ippon kumite—one step sparring, typically used for self defence drills
- Sanbon kumite—three step sparring, typically used to develop speed, strength, and technique
- Kiso kumite—structured sparring drawn from kata applications
- Jiyu kumite—free sparring

Basic Footwork

- *Nusumi ashi*—back foot steps in first, front foot steps second to close distance
- *Okuri ashi*—front foot steps in first to close distance, back foot follow
- *Tsugi ashi*—stutter step, typically the front foot makes a small closing step followed by a much larger one to close distance with the back foot following as needed
- *Ayu shi*—the back foot steps through to the front to close distance

Dojo Kun (The Code of Karate)

Karate has a *dojokun* which is basically a set of guidelines for karate-ka's to follow both in the dojo(a room in which Karate is taught) and out of the dojo, in a karate-ka's everyday life.

- Strive for perfection of character
- Be faithful to the Art, and train hard and safely
- Respect others, and refrain from violent behaviour

There are many ways to say this, depending on the Organisation, School or Instructor who teaches Karate.

Kokoro (The Student's Attitude)

Kokoro is a concept that is present through a great number of martial arts, but has no single absolute meaning and is actually quite difficult to translate from Japanese. This can be the case for many languages, but particularly so in Japanese (and also in Chinese in relation to Kung Fu and Tai Chi).

So you should strive to understand the movements and Katas you learn in the context of the original language it relates to. You may not understand it fully, but an appreciation of the language would be desirable, because it would of course serve to enhance your understanding of your martial art.

In this given context, *Kokoro,* means something like "heart," "character," or "attitude." *Character* is a central concept in Karate, and in keeping with the *do* or *way* nature of Karate in the modern age, there is a great emphasis on improving yourself which is not limited to the Art in itself—you should aim to improve yourself and be thoroughly dedicated in every key area of your life.

Unlike very aggressive styles of fighting such as Wing Chun Kung Fu, or Tae Kwon Do, for example, *Karate* is more for self-defence; not injuring one's opponent is the highest expression of the art. Some popularly repeated quotes implicating this concept include:

"The ultimate aim of Karate lies not in victory or defeat, but in the perfection of the character of its participants."—Gichin Funakoshi

There is a heavy emphasis on discipline, respect and structure which you as a Karate-ka will become familiar with from your first lesson.

Rei (The Ritual Bow in Karate, and Demonstration of Respect)

Rei—the ritual bow which all karate-ka must do before entering a dojo, leaving the dojo, and when practising with students in class.

If you are to truly follow the 'way of Karate', you must be courteous and show respect to others, not only in training but in your daily life as well.

While humble and gentle, you should never be too timid or restrained. Your performance in kata, whether basic, intermediate or advanced, should reflect your boldness, clarity and confidence.

This combination of boldness and gentleness leads ultimately to a worthy goal, one of harmony. It is true, as Master Funakoshi used to say, that the spirit of Karate would be lost without courtesy.

I found that Shotokan was a great style to learn initially, but I found Wado Ryu style more suitable for me. That said, I am more senior in the former, simply because I have studied it for longer. Sometimes you just find the right style for you, and in my case Shotokan, with its long stances and powerful shots, was great—but Wado Ryu, with its more upright style, plus faster techniques, combined with elements of JuJitsu in the system, was far more dynamic a style for me. Again, you need to find the right style that works for you.

Wado Ryu Karate was founded by Hironori Otsuka and I have studied it since 1993. Otsuka was one of the first students to be awarded black belt by Gichin Funakoshi, although he had trained with other Karate masters before him.

I found Wado Ryu style more suitable for me than Shotokan style perhaps because the emphasis was on:-

- A higher, more upright stance
- Ball of the foot work rather than heel
- Body twisting (more emphasis on hip movement)
- Inclusion of JuJitsu (a separate art in itself but complements Wado Ryu perfectly)

My Karate syllabus has nine *kyu*—or student—gradings, before reaching the first dan grade (black belt). So initially it would seem to be an easier system than my Kung Fu syllabus, which has eighteen gradings for which a student needs to take in order to reach black sash.

This of course could not be further from the truth though, and the Karate system I instruct is very tough and will examine every part of a student's ability and character, and of course make them a very well rounded and able fighter.

Closing chapter notes: *A student who is trained well in Karate will be a competent fighter, even when compared to other styles. Certain styles have their limitations, which is why Wado Ryu is so good (JuJitsu is part of the system) and I would encourage those interested in Karate to seek out a teacher proficient in this style.*

12

Jeet Kune Do

Use 'no way' as 'the' way.

Chapter focus: *Jeet Kune Do was created out Bruce Lee's need to unify certain fighting styles, and to simplify what he thought was the unnecessary parts in Wing Chun Kung Fu. Students should not take on Jeet Kune Do practice lightly. As you will see in this chapter, Jeet Kune Do is not 'Wing Chun plus' or 'Wing Chun lite'.*

I want to set out at the start that whilst Bruce Lee saw things in Wing Chun he didn't like, he still saw the merits of the system and so made Wing Chun the foundation of his system.

It is not a hybrid system. More accurately, it could be said to be a conceptual style rather than a fully fledged Art in itself. This is perhaps why I myself do not teach a 'belted' system. Instead, a student must reach proficiency ranks, of which there are five in my system.

Whilst many of you may choose to start Jeet Kune Do training because of Bruce Lee, you must remember that Jeet Kune Do was a system devised by and built for one man's methodology and physiology.

I strongly believe that Bruce Lee wanted people to learn elements of the style without actually copying him move-for-move. Martial artists of any style should therefore learn the system well that their teacher gives to them, but express it in their own individual manner. Use 'no way' as 'the' way.

Bruce Lee, the founder of *Jeet Kune Do*, The Way of the Intercepting Fist . . . never learnt the whole system of Wing Chun Kung Fu, but he certainly saw its merits. He famously says in '*Enter the Dragon*' that his 'style' could be called 'the art of fighting without fighting'.

While that is true to some extent, I think it is the simplicity of his intercepting style, that makes it so appealing, and crucially, so effective.

There are no real belts to attain, or forms to learn, The style is, what it is: a convergence of many styles with Wing Chun Kung Fu at its core.

Because of this, it should not be interpreted or simplified as 'Wing Chun Plus' or 'Wing Chun—Lite'—far from it. It is a system born out of the best of Wing Chun, with the free flowing movement and lack of fixed positions that, perhaps even I can accept, places *some* limits on Wing Chun as a fighting system.

But there and right there, the criticism, such as it is, ends.

The literal meaning is 'the Way of the Intercepting Fist'. I interpret it more as 'the way of the intercepting technique' because it could be the fist, or could be a leg technique, or it could be a intercepting block like the bon sao against a punch, then striking towards the opposite side of the face.

Jeet Kune Do differs from other martial arts in the sense of:

- No fixed positions and no 'classical' forms
- Free flowing fighting movement
- Blindingly fast speed rarely equalled by other styles

When you read the above, you may think *'Oh! Everyone must want to study this!'*

The reality is, there are very few Jeet Kune Do teachers, and even less are the good Jeet Kune Do teachers . . . and so, there are not so many good Jeet Kune Do students out there.

This is a shame because the system has great advantages over others. I don't wish to get into the argument / debate of 'which style is best?' . . . that question is most easily answered by 'whoever is best at their particular style, on any given day'.

As aforementioned it is a system that has Wing Chun at its core. So if you have no grounding in martial arts, you might just find Jeet Kune Do rather difficult to pick up, at least in the early months of training.

If a student has a grounding in martial arts, and specifically—the art of Wing Chun Kung Fu style, then it will be much easier to pick Jeet Kune Do up.

You will notice I have not so far abbreviated the system to 'JKD'—the more popular way to say it. Nor would I do this with Tae-Kwon-Do and abbreviate to TKD.

There are already too many acronyms in the world already and so I do not wish to add to them. So I will call this style Jeet Kune Do.

Does learning Jeet Kune Do mean I will learn to fight like Bruce Lee?

This style, like all styles you are inspired by, allows you to express yourself in the way that suits you best. Unless you are to become some kind of Bruce Lee clone, which in itself is no bad thing, you won't be able to fight like him.

If Jeet Kune Do is so great, why doesn't everyone do it?

There are many reasons for this. It is not an easy style for beginners to pick up. It is not so widely taught, compared to Karate or kick boxing. Many get frustrated that they cannot learn to fight like, or punch as fast as Bruce Lee. For that reason alone, be inspired by but forget about Bruce—at least in this context.

Should I learn Jeet Kune Do at a school with a proper syllabus and belt award system?

In answering the first part of that question, I say yes, absolutely. As to the second part, one cannot learn to fight like, or punch as fast as Bruce Lee. For that reason alone, be inspired by him by all means, but become the fighter you want to become by expressing your Jeet Kune Do in your way. Again, look at the sub-header to this chapter—*use no way as the way.*

Some schools place too much emphasis on the merits of awarding belts their system, however Bruce Lee was adamant that his style would not be corrupted like other styles. That is not to say a system with belt awards incorporated into it is not worth anything, it is just the way of things in many clubs today, especially in the West.

Jeet Kune Do is comprehensive art, although it is best deployed by using the simplicity of it to devastating effect. So—keep things simple. Learn the system, but do not be limited by the system. It has no limits. In fact, *no art* has limits. It is only limited by the imagination, or lack of imagination of the instructor.

Some instructors would have you believe that the 'syllabus is the syllabus', and that is it. Of course the syllabus is there to guide you along, help you attain new levels of proficiency and so forth, but the good instructor will be able to explain how each technique, or set of techniques, reveals themselves in new ways.

Stances

Adopt a semi-crouch stance in order to be in the most effective position to strike your opponent. Bruce Lee called this the 'small phasic bent-knee stance'.

You may have heard that in true Jeet Kune Do there are no stances . . . well this is not true, as you have to have a stance of some sort.

This is what we mean by the 'small phasic bent-knee stance'.

This semi-crouch stance is perfect for fighting because you are relaxed but are, at all times, very alert, and in a comfortable balanced position from which you can attack, counter or defend without preliminary movement. It is also more realistic in combat unlike other classical stances where they imitate the posture of an animal (horse stance, cat stance) or some other object (bow and arrow). If you will notice, the bai-jong more closely resembles a boxer's on-guard stance.

The Jeet Kune Do *bai-jong* is also referred as the *small phasic bent knee stance.*

Small

This means what is actually appropriate, not over-extended steps nor an insufficient length of step or positioning. Small, quick and accurate are vital for speed, and controlled balance in bridging the gap to your opponent.

Phasic

This is a stage or interval in the development of the so-called stance—it is not still or static, but is ever and constantly changing, which is how your fighting style should be.

Bent-Knee Position

This ensures readiness in movement at all times.

The distance of your feet is a natural step apart—that is to say, what is a natural step apart *for you*.

Do not place your stance too small and certainly not over-extended. The heel of your rear foot is raised an inch while the heel of your lead foot is ever-so-slightly touching the ground. Your lead elbow should be positioned just three inches from your body.

The Head

The most important part of your body perhaps will avoid blows by bobbing and weaving.

The head should be treated as if it were part of the trunk of the body, generally, with no independent motion of its own. In close contact fighting, it should be carried vertically with the point of the chin pinned to the collarbone and the side of the chin held against the inside of the lead shoulder. In this way, you will keep the chin out of harm's way, and make the rest of your head very difficult to hit.

The chin does not go all the way down to meet the lead shoulder, nor does the lead shoulder come all the way up. They meet at the optimum point, which is halfway. The shoulder is raised slightly and your chin should be tucked in, but not too tight, otherwise your fluidity and movement will be restricted.

If you do tuck your chin into the lead shoulder too much or far too tight it will turn your neck into a very unnatural and very uncomfortable position.

Only on extreme defensive measures should you use this position, but you have to ask yourself how you got yourself in to this weak position in the first place.

The Primary Leads:

The Lead Shoulder

This should be slightly raised and your chin slightly lowered to protect your chin and part of your face on the lower right side of the body.

The lead shoulder must at all times be relaxed and loose—a good maxim for all martial arts and fighting preparation actually. By doing this, you will be able to snap your lead arm, perhaps the jabbing motion, super fast and in repeated bursts of energy if required. The shoulder is also used to protect the chin in the act of close-quarter combat, just do not raise it so high in a way that you block your view.

The Lead Hand

You will rely heavily on your lead attacks, be they with your legs or hands. For your lead hand specifically, it serves to protect your face and your groin, two very vital areas of your body, so work hard to improve the ability of your lead hand, in attack, interception and defence.

The lead hand must be loose, relaxed, slightly lower than your lead shoulder, and always poised to attacking. If your shoulder is relaxed and loose, you will be able to snap your lead extremely fast. If you are always tense, or even sometimes tense, try the same technique again. You will find it will not work!

You must always keep your lead hand in a slight weaving motion to keep your opponent guessing and counter guessing—make the opponent make the wrong guess.

The lead hand can be in any of the following positions:

Low-line position

The low-line position is preferred because most people are weak at low-line defence. It also prevents your lead arm from making contact with your opponent's for a possible immobilisation of them, or more simply, how to lock them up and stop them using their legs and their arms.

Adapting the low-line position makes your head open for an attack but you can get around this by making your head a moving target.

The Lead Forearm

Defends your midsection and the ribcage.

The lead forearm must at all times protect your midsection area especially your solar plexus, but also the lower part of your stomach. The position of the forearm is dictated by the position of your lead hand and lead elbow.

The Lead Elbow

This defends the midsection and the right side of your body.

The lead elbow is also used to nullify your opponent's attack. For example, as your opponent delivers a side kick, instead of parrying the blow with your lead hand or rear hand you can use your lead elbow to hit your opponent's attacking foot or arm. Of course, timing is critical to this technique's success.

Lead Knee

This is slightly turned inward to defend the groin area.

The position of the lead knee and of the lead foot dictates the position of the trunk. If the lead foot and legs are in the correct position, the trunk automatically assumes the proper position.

Lead Foot

Place this at a 25 to 30 degree angle. It is your primary attack tool for kicking and 'stop-kick' movement.

In Jeet Kune Do, the lead foot is used mostly for kicking but also blocking with stop-hits, the opponent's techniques. The position of the lead foot depends on your strategy.

My Jeet Kune Do students will debate on how the lead foot must be positioned in order to be in the optimum position for striking. My preference is to turn the lead foot ever-so-slightly inward for defence whilst continually assessing the opponent's move and turning it slightly outward in preparation for an attack or counter-attack.

The lead foot must also bear about a third of your body weight for rapid attacks and counters.

Rear Side

Rear

Heavily depended on for defence. It protects your face plus your groin.

The open palm of your rear hand must face the opponent and is positioned between the opponent and the rear shoulder, in line with the lead shoulder. The rear hand may also rest *lightly* upon the body—note the emphasis on lightly. The arm should be relaxed and easy, ready to attack or defend.

As with the lead hand, the rear hand may perform a circular weaving motion. This can confuse the opponent, which is exactly what we want to achieve. It makes it all the easier to defeat them.

Rear Forearm

Defends the mid-section of the body.

The rear forearm covers the solar plexus area. The position of the rear forearm is dictated by the position of the rear hand and rear elbow.

Rear Elbow

This defends the left side of your body.
The rear elbow is held down and in front of the short ribs.

Rear Foot

This is placed at a 45 to 50 degree angle and the heel is slightly raised for greater mobility. It has to be ready to fire up your body forward like a coiled spring to ensure a lightning response through the elasticity of the technique.

The rear foot must bear 65 to 70% of your body weight.

The bai-jong stance is the basic primary fighting posture of a Jeet Kune Do fighter. Although the above statements are true it must not be taken as the absolute truth, with no room for manouevre.

When it comes to total combat, it really doesn't matter what posture you are in, what lead you are in (left lead or right lead), and so on and so forth. Remember that there are four ranges of combat:-

Kicking, punching, trapping and grappling. You cannot continue to stay so rigid in the bai-jong stance while trapping due to the nature this range. You must use anything that works.

It is the same as when you attack the centre line . . . if you meant to hit left when you hit right, so long as it lands, or you are in a position to defend your opponent's attack, who is to say what you did is wrong? Attack the centre, and guard it with your life. That is the way to success in fighting.

Closing chapter notes: *Jeet Kune Do is one of the purest fighting styles there is. To make it work in practise you need to get theories working for you.*

John Hennessy

Theories are just that—so if you cannot defeat your opponent by putting theory into practise, what's the point?

There are so many scenarios you could potentially find yourself in that even in one book would be hard to include them all. So the best approach is often the simplest one. I would ask my students to come up with a situation that maybe I have not covered. In fairness to me, I have seen a lot over the years and so am not afraid to include it in my lessons. But I accept someone may come along and say to me 'yes, but what if THIS happened?'

So you have to make it work in practise. Many theories bite the dust as soon as they are tested. I would never foolishly make a 100% guarantee that students who use the techniques I show and teach them, will work in all of the situations, all of the time.

I do say, however, that the objective should be to 'get home safely' and in order to do this, the first steps are not fancy martial arts techniques—it is more likely to be something much more important.

Many good martial artists are undone by the one who is more aware of what is going on. If you are so 'tunnel-visioned' that you can only see what is in front of you, what if it is not that which is the problem, but something else?

In essence, try to continually assess what is going on during a fight and be wary of an opponent who can vary his attacking methods and approach. The competent Jeet Kune Do fighter can do this with relative ease, and this makes him a most unsettling fighter to compete with.

13

Why people take up martial arts, why some can't stay at it

Chapter focus: *You often hear that there are two types of things, but in relation to martial arts, whilst there are mostly two types of student, you can't be so generalist on this. You cannot expect everyone to be like the instructor, although each student could reflect the instructor in themselves, to some small degree. Ultimately they should express an improved form of themselves.*

Why certain people can see things through, and others often give up at the first hurdle—or first difficult hurdle is difficult to understand.

In my experience of teaching over the years, I learned to quickly assess who was messing me about, and who was serious about training with me.

It is not easy to do martial arts, or to do anything worthwhile. But too many give up, too soon. Or are unrealistic about their progress about two or three lessons into their training.

The chapter is for those then, who have perhaps done martial arts in the past and for whatever reason, gave it up, or never even started.

Far too often there are excuses made by those who don't make it to their goal, and this unfortunately is not just limited to martial arts, but to their lives in general. Most of it, unfortunately, is of their own making. Too many times it has become convenient to find a reason not to attend a lesson they themselves have booked. Some even are deluded in the sense that 'they know better than the instructor' . . . so why bother to train with him then?

Such students are not going to last. Point of fact, this is why many teachers do not wish to be bothered teaching personal training. Some students don't have the stomach for it, and this is exactly what my first instructor told me all those years ago.

She told me very clearly 'If we start, we do not stop. If we do stop, it's because one or both of us are dead. But, aside from that small detail, we don't stop.'

My first instructor had a never-ending supply of wry jokes, but it was often hard to tell if she really was joking or not. So it was always best to be cautious with that.

Of course, I wanted to be the best I could be. I could not have truly known how hard it would be at that time. I just thought it would be something I could bear with, and by the end of it, should it actually have an 'end', I'd be somewhere between half-decent and very decent at martial arts.

For others, they rarely have a singular focus on anything. These people, or others like them, cannot see to attend training if their friend / brother / dog can't come with them. This is a falsehood. If you train together you actually coast to each other's speed, you don't actually push yourself. Then, one night, you or your friend decide you don't want to go, and what happens is, the rot sets in. It sets in slowly, or at a quicker pace. But it definitely sets in.

Some wake up on January 1st each year and decide they are going to change their life for the better. While it is no doubt an admiral concept, it is highly unworkable one. This is not a pessimistic view of mine, but more a realistic one bore out of experience with such people.

The reasons for this spectacular lack of achievement is obvious, if you think about it for a moment. If you have been living your life a certain way for a certain (usually a long) period of time, it is extremely hard, in fact nigh-on impossible to change overnight. Maybe, it lasts for a day or two. Perhaps a week. You may, through some set of circumstances, get through to February and still be working on this amazing life change. Such people are in the minority though.

Quitting smoking is an obvious and all too common one. However there are people who do it—and perhaps decide on 31st December of the previous year that 'this is the last one' . . . and so it turns out to be the case. Good for them.

Martial arts—forget the style for a moment—is not something you just up and decide to do. This is something that takes a lifetime of dedication to get good at. And—there has to be a very, very good reason for doing it.

Sometimes you will get inspired. You'll see Bruce Lee in *Fist of Fury* knocking out all comers in that famous scene in the Karate dojo. Jet Li and Donnie Yen facing off in *Once Upon a Time in China 2*, or Jackie Chan in *Drunken Master*. Yuen Biao in the *Prodigal Son*. See a film, be inspired to do something positive as a result of it, is all well and good. For most, such things turn out to be false inspirations and were just the 'fad' at the time. As time passes, so does the novelty. A pity.

Once you've seen these films though, you'll be high kicking your way towards a black belt, won't you?

If this sounds too basic, think about each time you've seen Rocky Balboa training . . . Haven't you just made a bee-line to the nearest gym, or long for a long hard run? Of course you have.

Again, it is to be commended. Any exercise is good. And anything that inspires exercise, is a good thing.

So with so much inspiration about, why do people quit the training? A lot of the problem is in the unrealistic expectations of people. Some of these may be familiar to you, whether you are an instructor or a student. Whichever side you find yourself on, you may see something familiar about the following statements.

"I want to be a black belt."

That is a fine goal. Don't we all aspire to be a black belt?. Getting a black belt is an admirable achievement, provided you have had to work for it and new belts haven't just been handed to you like candy bars every few months. Turning up for lessons is one thing. Working hard in-between lessons is another.

The system that you are doing shouldn't just be punches, kicks and forms. It should be embedded in reality. It shouldn't be something you do when you turn up for class. You should do it constantly, be thinking about it even when you are not physically practicing it. And so, the exercises are one thing. You need them in order that your muscles work properly for the more vigorous techniques you will be undertaking.

You should be able to see the syllabus for the level you are trying to attain.

You should be able to ask the instructor anything about the system, and he or she should be able to answer it. In addition, you should not be frightened or concerned to ask for the instructors credentials, provided in part by certificates from his masters or credible insurance including public liability and professional indemnity. It is fair to say this request should be done early on in your training.

"I want to lose weight."

Losing weight is often a by-product of 'good' training. If you find the right program for you, you will most likely lose weight, which anyone will agree is a good thing. The key thing though, is not to lose weight by itself—it should be to lose the weight and keep it off.

Some will try more than one technique, such as controlling their diet. Some try to do this in an extreme manner though. For example, students may attempt to 'binge-starve' themselves, which is not good, given that this self-induced starvation, along with trying to do exercise at the same time. I have always believed you can eat pretty much what you want. Anything is fine, in moderation of course.

You should not overdo anything. You should not give yourself a false sense of security, in that you trained for four hours when in fact what you did was *allocate a time to train of four hours*, but for the most part were taking lengthy breaks in-between your repetitions. Just who are you trying to kid?

It would be far better to train for one hour, to an absolute maximum of ninety minutes to two hours and stick to that regime, as rigidly as you can. The reason for this is that if you try to do too much things too quickly, or in too big a way (so much so that it becomes unmanageable) the worst thing that can happen to anyone is 'burn out'.

"I saw '*Enter the Dragon*' and want to fight like Bruce Lee."

As aforementioned, being inspired by a master or a great martial arts actor is a great thing. The point is, once you have been inspired, to keep it in check, in the realms of reality.

Bruce Lee is shown performing a somersault over a group of martial artists near the start of the film. A great move. Can you do it? No? Do you think if you train for a few months, you'll be able to do it? If your instructor told you it was possible, but you had to train for a year and train several hard hours a week, could you? No?? You are not alone on this.

Many lack the 'stomach', 'brains' and maturity to do martial arts techniques, especially those techniques that look good and so take much more time and discipline to learn.

Getting a black belt, as quick as possible, and not caring which way you go about it.

Most schools and instructors have teaching martial arts as their livelihood. They charge for lessons, suits, gradings, licenses, club merchandise and so on.

When a student starts dropping off, or challenges the instructor as to when he might be allowed to grade, how do instructors manage keep them coming to the school?

Instructors are hoping that he won't go off and train with some other teacher of a McDojo where producing masses of black belts (but the quality and standard is poor) is the norm.

Or perhaps they read something in one of the main martial arts publications, and see an advertisement for 'get your black belt in just 12 months', this can be very eye-catching for those who are not really interested in the true way of martial arts.

All that consumes such a person is getting that black belt. Just go buy one then if that's all it means to you !! But don't think you would able to go up against a black belt. Or even yellow belt for that matter. Bring a gun. Then maybe you have a chance. But you've lost the argument for your case there and then.

The character of those who stick at it.

These people decide they really want to achieve something of true value in their lives. For many, the realisation of passing the first grade is a tremendous achievement. Get one under your belt, it is likely many more will follow, provided you work hard, stick at the syllabus, and accept that you will have your good lessons and not-so-good, like when you have good days and off days. It happens.

The sensible approach is one where you can just forget about it and move on. Sometimes people over-analyse things, like 'why did he progress before me . . . I can beat him up!' . . . that's not really the point. The best competition is that which you provide for yourself, is yourself. Set yourself as the benchmark and aim to improve with each grading, sparring session, form practise, and basic technique.

I have not compared myself to anyone else and I never will . . . and it is not something I encourage students to do either.

14

Exploding the Myths of Martial Arts

*If your opponent is right in front of you,
do you really need to run up walls?*

Chapter focus: *There is a lot of nonsense in martial arts. The mythology and legend building seems to be something some in martial arts circles want to uphold. I have no interest in that.*

This chapter is a reality check for those who buy into this all too easily. That is not to say students are a little naive, far from it. But maybe they have never been told what is really true, and what is not.

There are many myths surrounding martial arts. Some may relate to the apparent invincibility of a particular student, teacher, or actor. This could be to do with how they lived, trained or died.

Whatever the individual case, you can only really deal with the truth. So that is where I'll begin.

Myths about instructors.

In training with some of my instructors over the years, I found they had an aura about them or a presence, which certainly felt very real.

This automatically gave them the upper hand I felt, and so I believed that no matter what I would do, they could not be beaten during sparring, or in some cases, have a single guard broken down or strike landed on them.

You have to remember that instructors, even those truly great ones who have deservedly attained the title of 'Master' are human. It is just a simple case that they have trained for a very long time, and when doing so, with diligence, focus and hard discipline.

If you apply the same methods to your training, is it probable you could attain this air of invincibility? It is, but you have to be aware of what you are getting into, and the dedication required is more than some can ever hope to achieve. This is not only on the mere practical side of learning your syllabus extremely well. Some very good exponents of their Art simply are not meant to become instructors. I actually believe that some students get 'pushed' into a role they are rarely ready for, and it is also interesting that some schools have instructors teaching classes where the students have a higher grade than they do.

The good teacher will go about their business quietly, and unlike the popular myth that all instructors do in class is 'shout, point and criticise', not all do, and in fact many rarely raise their voice, and will act in a genteel way and with humility.

I would encourage anyone who reads this book to seek out such an instructor, because they will not only teach you the good values of martial arts, but in such a way that this spills over in every area of your life.

You may think this is a contradiction in the sense that I wrote at the start of the book about some of the training methods Sifu Li put me through. You have to remember she was very young to be an instructor, but I have little doubt she was one of the very best I ever had the privilege to train with. She just wanted me to be good, and I had a very tough learning curve.

Again I have to say she rarely raised her voice, to me, or to anyone else. If anyone had an air of invincibility about them, it was her. She made it nigh on impossible for me to land shots on her, but I realised actually when training with others or competing, just how effective this method of training was. I was becoming a better fighter all the time, when I was feeling demoralised from the fact I could not even get near her. I think in seven years I landed one clean shot on her, but would land several on virtually anybody else.

Myths about 'this style is better than anything else'.

I am sometimes asked what is my favourite martial art or style. It is a difficult question to answer because so many styles suits so many different purposes.

The question could perhaps be re-phrased as 'what is the best style of fighting for the given situation?'

I believe the best style, is one that suits you. No one style can assume superiority over another . . . the superiority in itself is down to the student, his teacher, the merits of the syllabus, how hard, and how often he practises.

I have seen enough over the years to know the merits of Kung Fu over Karate, of Chen Tai Chi over Yang style, of Karate over Kung Fu . . . and it can go on and on.

Ultimately the student is the one who presents the best of the style with the best expression of his ability. If good enough, during a fight, it is this student who will prevail.

That's why this ongoing debate will never be resolved, much like the individual fighters debate on 'who would win between Bruce Lee or Jackie Chan' or 'Jet Li or Donnie Yen'? . . . and so on.

Does it really matter?

Myths about the 'black belt' equals 'expert'.

Black belts have reached a good standard in their Art. How good they are, compared to other black belts, from other Schools, is open to interpretation.

When I reached my first black belt, I actually didn't feel as elated as I thought I would. Sure, I had worked hard on the system and for many years too. But I still felt a bit of a cheat, in that I really did not think I had deserved such an accolade.

However, I came to accept and understand that actually, it was all a new beginning and I would re-learn everything again, in a whole new way.

Of course I would learn new skills along the way to my second dan black belt, but I think many, many years would pass before I would consider myself an expert.

Myths about the anything less than black belt equals 'novice'.

Some of the best fighters I came across were not actually black belts and whilst that may sound strange, I still believe this to be the case.

For instance, let's say you tell someone you practise martial arts, and they happen not to practise it, they will want to know 'So ! Are you a black belt then?' Let us say you are a yellow belt, and you tell them so. In many cases they will look at you like you are nothing, and that even they, the unskilled ones, could beat you up.

Maybe that is harsh, but it is just the view in society that you are expected to be at this great level, almost instantly.

People who train in martial arts know that each belt really is earned, and if they can convey the merits of each level to those who ask, progress to avoid this popular misconception will be achieved.

Martial arts movies have some great examples of wushu, others less so. But some are so impressed by the 'fantasy' element they actually think such things are in 'normal' every day practise of martial arts. They wonder why a 'master', who has been practising martial arts all these years cannot or will not do these feats for the on-looking students.

The problem, at least for the so-called students that want to see this sort of thing, is that the instructor is not there to provide parlour tricks for the students. The instructor is there to run a lesson. End of story. Instructor says, student does. That is not brainwashing, it is part of the discipline.

Of course you can question the instructor, and the good ones should not mind the odd question. But unless you are asked to in the lesson, leave the questions until after the lesson, and also if the instructor has time for your questions.

If the instructor doesn't provide the tricks for students, especially those who are impressed by such things, then those students will soon be off doing something else. That is, ultimately, a good thing.

An instructor only wants good, hard working students in the class . . . otherwise he will be spending his time on those who are disruptive to the other students. The instructor has little time to get round the whole class, so if some are going to mess about, it is best they are not there at all.

In addition, disciplining such students sets the tone and standards for the lesson—the instructor is not there to baby-sit young children. He has a lesson to teach.

In one such instance with Sifu Li, Karen literally threw a student out of her class. What happened was, the student kept quizzing Karen, and actually challenged her to some techniques he had learned from another instructor (apparently).

She quietly said it was a Karate class, and his 'other skills' had no place here and could he just focus on the Karate training.

He did as she said for a few minutes anyway. When it came to sparring, Karen paired us all off against each other, and on the second round she was paired off with this guy. He repeatedly tried to take her down with the other stuff he learned. She stopped him once and asked him only to use Karate.

He then swore at her, at which point she threw him over her head, and he landed some 15 feet away, *outside* of the training area. Calmly, following him outside, she saw he had gashed his head on the reception desk. She patched him up and told him to go to the hospital to get it checked out, and to never darken her school's door again.

Was this too harsh? Could you really say she overreacted?

There are some prospective wannabe black belts that take Kung Fu films all too seriously. Whilst much of the content, particularly in the 1980s flicks and some of in the 1990s were really over the top, by the mid 1990s things were improving. It is a sad state of affairs that *Enter the Dragon* was still considered the best martial arts movie around, twenty years after its release.

I am all for people watching movies and being impressed by them to the extent that they want to study martial arts to a great level. The key bit here is, the moves you see on the big screen (in many films, not all of course) are to some extent, completely unrealistic and totally impractical in the real world.

For those moves that actually are realistic and practical, you have to remember that these moves are scripted and choreographed to make the main actors look good. Of course they are good martial artists anyway, but don't expect how they do it in the movie to translate exactly to the real world.

It just doesn't work like in real life. That is why it is called a movie !!

There are some films that do try and show real martial arts and it would be those I myself would have an interest in, but to recommend films to students? No, far better to let them seek out a film and watch it. If it is good, learn what you can from it.

However, it is pure folly to watch a film and expect to be able to copy the moves you see even if you practised every day, for hours on end, starting from scratch.

To those that may view that as a rather defeatist attitude, I would say to them 'do you really want to learn the true quality martial arts, or some flashy moves that will end up accomplishing nothing?'

To the group of you who agree with the first part of that statement, you would be welcome to train with me. To the group of you who agree with the latter part of that statement, ask yourself could you really see yourself defending yourself or someone you know with 'flashy moves?' I don't think so.

This is because true martial arts are not flashy, or for show. They have a quality, a real kick about them that is not present in other so-called flashy martial arts. For those of you who have gotten to this part of the book, you will know what I am on about.

You will also know the mind-set of those who start martial arts, and stick at it—and those who start, and quickly give up.

That is why this book is called the 'essence' of martial arts, because it deals with the immediate things you need to know, or should know.

I do not expect every one to turn into the perfect student as soon as they have finished reading this book. But those that have read it, should at least begin to understand what tools they need in order to defend themselves and others, and what path they should take in order that their martial arts life is not spend on fruitless tasks.

For example, like knowing how many punches you can do in one second, or if you can copy a difficult move you saw in a film once.

What is important is only this—can you do what you need to do, when you need to do it?

It concentrates on the quality aspect, and not the wishy-washy, useless styles that have pervaded the martial arts arena (especially in the last twenty years or so).

Brute force. That does not often, or usually win the day. I have fought many people who were twice my size or weight, or just plain aggressive, and defeated them. How did I manage this? If you are the kind of fighter who'goes in' extremely hard, you put so much power behind it, that is fine if it connects with your opponent's body, but what if it doesn't? What will you do then?

This is no slate at those who work out at the gym. I think any exercise is a good thing and is to be encouraged and applauded. However, a martial artist needs to use the muscle groups in a different way, and just trying to power your way through, especially against an opponent with superior skill, will simply not work.

There are many schools that advocate the 'breaking of wooden blocks' in order to prove a student's worthiness for promotion to a senior belt.

While this in itself is not a 'myth to explode' you have to wonder why it is that some schools think the ability to break a wooden block would make you a competent fighter. Yes, it may be exciting to do or watch, but cold realisation would tell you that it is utterly meaningless.

Bruce Lee uttered an often quoted line in '*Enter the Dragon*' the line being 'Boards don't hit back' (after O'Hara breaks one just before he and Lee start fighting). That was in a movie of course, but Lee himself probably understood that circus tricks alone would not win you a fight.

The myth of 'speed' or 'he's faster than me'. That is not the case either. It is all down to technical ability. Speed is a factor, just as power is a factor, but the key equation is as follows:-

$$ABILITY = technique + speed + power$$

Look at that equation as a whole for a second and you will come to realise that if you leave out of of those components, you will lack the ability to strike your opponent when you need to. Now look at that equation again. It is what has worked for me during all of my martial arts training.

So go and practise. You have still a lot to learn.

15

Tournaments and Street Fighting for Real

Putting it all together.

Chapter focus: *In this final chapter, emphasis will be put on how you actually should go about putting the skills you learn in class, into an actual, useful practical way.*

You will soon realise that how you use your skills in tournaments, and how you would need to use them in the real world when faced with a life-threatening situation, are not related. There are key differences, and those will be expanded on in this chapter.

It is rather fitting then that this be the concluding chapter of this book.

I found I needed different strategies whether it was a tournament or fighting to save myself in a real life situation. Read the following chapter based on my real-life experiences, and get from it what is important to you.

Using martial arts to save your life.

Let me talk about the real life situation because I think ultimately, that is why everyone should take up and stick to learning a martial art well. In my experience people I have talked to have maybe studied martial arts for possibly six months at the most, and think they will be able to handle any given situation. I can tell you, no matter how progressive the School syllabus is or how great your teacher is . . . six months in all probability will not be enough.

I had been fortunate to be some way into my martial arts training when I had been attacked by two youths at a shopping centre close to my then home, which was in a rough part of the city.

It was partly my own error that the youths in question were able to get close to me. I was wearing earphones because I was listening to music on my personal stereo.

It was my own lack of awareness that made my situation worse than perhaps it could have been.

The two youths approached me, one waving his arms to get my attention. He was asking me if I 'had a light' and I said no, that I didn't smoke, and went to carry on with my approach through the subway.

He said to me 'where are you going?' and put his hand on my shoulder. He then demanded money from me, whilst his 'colleague' produced a flick knife and placed it near my rib cage.

There wasn't really time to be frightened. It was the first time I had been in this sort of situation and I could only say that it felt surreal.

I couldn't really help the youth with his demands, as I actually had no money on me at all, and I wondered what his reaction would be when I would tell him so. I thought he would be disappointed, to put it mildly, but I was more concerned with his friend who had the knife at my side. I was wearing a really thick leather coat at the time, and thinking it was a good idea *'it will take him a while to cut through that, with that little knife'* I mused.

You've got to understand that this was all happening at a hundred miles per second. I had to answer quick, think quick, and 'do' quick, otherwise I could end up a bloody mess on the floor, rotting away in the subway until someone found me and alerted the authorities.

My first thought was to hit the guy with the knife. I thought to use a back fist strike, or in Karate, an *uraken,* to his head. If I hit him hard enough, I reckoned the artex wall behind him would serve as a double-hit, and I could run under the guy whose arm was pinning me to the wall by my shoulder.

My second thought was to think 'no, stall for time, give them what you've got' . . . but I knew I had less than a pound in change in my pocket. I doubted that would satisfy them.

So I went for my third thought . . . which was my first thought, and swung my fist as fast and as hard as I could, right at the knife-wielder's head.

Boom. He hit that wall hard, and I am sure I drew heavy blood from him.

The taller guy was I think a bit shocked because he momentarily relaxed the pressure on my shoulder. I wasted no time in swiping his arm away, and running for it.

Having the time over again, I could have still been attacked even if I had not been wearing my earphones because my route to home was through that subway.

It has since been 'filled in' by the local authorities, and I hope no-one else suffers an attack like that.

The experience left me shook up, but thinking that I had survived it to fight another day, I made a promise to myself to be absolutely ready if it ever happened again.

*   *   *

Nine years after this first event, I was at my mom's home one evening when I told her I was going down the road just to get some food from the local chip shop.

Within a hundred yards of leaving the house, I noticed three young men coming my way on the same side of the road.

Wary of the area anyway, I was alert, but relaxed. Of course, at this point I just see them as a group of lads, nothing more.

As we got closer one actually walked ahead of the other two, and was walking right in my way so that one of us would have to move to avoid a collision.

To this day I never understand why people act like this. You have lots of pavement available to you and yet you end up bashing shoulders. What is up with people who act like this? In today's world, have people just lost respect and got no manners? What a shame if that is the case.

I went to move out of his way. Not because I was frightened of him, but because I just felt then, and feel now, that is the right course of action.

To my not-altogether-big surprise, he mirrored my movement and went to intercept me.

I left my guard down, because I saw no weapon, and knew I could respond, hard and quickly, if I needed to.

His two friends were smirking, and he then told me 'you've found trouble'.

I didn't know what he meant by that, much less did I care. I just thought *'I have to break this guy if he tries anything silly'* and he went to punch me, or grab me. I don't know really what he was going to do. All I can tell you is what I did to him, in order to get myself out of that situation.

You see, when people worry about being attacked by a group, my thought process is this. They can only usually attack you one at a time, the 'group' attack is a rarity and so if this were to ever happen to you, and I sincerely hope not, try not to panic, for the reasons mentioned above.

I grabbed his arm with what must have seemed to him with alarming speed. I used a Wing Chun Larp Sao to grab his arm and followed it quickly with a side punch, hard into his ribs, which, at that short distance, allowed me to hit extremely powerfully, and I heard a crack as his rib cage gave way. I could have perhaps pulled the technique, but I thought I needed to disable him quickly in case his friends made a move towards me.

After that, it was easy to sweep his legs, which were now buckling, and as I took him to the ground, I placed one foot onto his chest, immobilising him.

Looking at his two friends, who by now had appropriately lost the smirks from their faces, I asked them if they wanted to end up like their friend.

To say that they looked scared was perhaps an understatement, and they turned tail and ran. So much for being thick as thieves.

I told the guy, who had told me a minute or so back that it was *me* who had 'found trouble', that I was going to step off him now and he would be wise not to follow me.

I promised to be less lenient next time, and to his friends if necessary, if he tried anything like that again.

Suffice to say, he didn't follow me and I carried on to the shop.

If at all possible, I do think it is best to be at a high state of awareness in these situations. It is not to say that even if you are, everything will go okay, but obviously, that is the hope—that you can actually walk away from the situation relatively unscathed.

Don't allow second doubts to creep in. As you saw in my first story, I was fortunate in that the first reaction happened to be the right one. I had nowhere to run, so had to deal with the situation. That, or face becoming just another statistic, another story in the press. I was extremely lucky that that was not to be my fate.

I also hope you never have to use your skills to save the life of either yourself, a loved one, or someone in trouble. But if you must, make sure it is you that comes through it okay. You didn't ask for the trouble, but you dealt with it. That is the best you can do. And perhaps the assailant will have learned something too—not to follow this life . . . because there is always someone tougher than you, and it is best not to up the chances of running into him.

*   *   *

Tournaments and Sparring

Sparring is important because it is in that instance that you can find out what works, and what does not.

Perhaps you use it to see how you react under pressure, because if you are always punching and kicking in the air, and without the resistance that an opponent would provide, you do not really know, for sure, that the techniques actually do work.

In my classes I teach only things that actually work, and I do not bother with superfluous things that are best left for 'show off' styles that have no practical real-life use. The balance between the Art you teach and the real Self Defence that you must teach is a fine one. As a teacher, one cannot place too heavy an emphasis on one or the other.

If you find yourself with such a teacher, you will be left wanting in a tournament or in a real life situation. And that is no good at all.

In my longer sparring classes, we do four rounds.

Round One is a general round, typically you will be using this to warm up, try different techniques with light application and reasonable speed, and try to take an opportunity or create one.

Round Two is where the student is often doing an all-out attack, and I would generally defend. But I would caution the student that they should still think of their defence, because even though I would not be punching or kicking, they could still be hit. The reason would be because I could still grab, punch, stamp and strike towards them.

Round Three is the counter attack round where the student would attack and I would counter with an attack of my own, which could be a single attack or several. Usually students find this a very hard round to deal with because they have to 'play their hand'—successfully, or the counter attack will cut them right open.

Round Four is like round one, only is executed at a much faster, harder, and tighter pace. This is more akin to real competitions where both fighters will be expected to really 'go for it' and not be just purely defensive, a strategy which is bound to lead to failure.

As someone who competed over a fourteen year period, I had just one reverse in the semi / full contact tournament circuit. I do not recognise non-contact tournaments as being based on real fighting, so will talk only about those which were well organised in my view, and based on actual fighting, in the sense of how it would play outside in the real world.

I was prepared to even get disqualified in one event of a particular tournament so that I could augment my strategy for the other. This was a risky strategy and I would not recommend it, and certainly if I had this period of my life over again, I would not do anything other than do my best to compete with honour, integrity, and humility.

In my early days of competition, having won my inaugural one with relative ease (also to my great surprise) I became perhaps a bit cocky, and a little too arrogant.

But I must explain that because if you read it so simply like that, you might believe I am actually like that, or was like that, back then.

Actually, it was a position I took driven by some fear. Not the fear that I would lose, although that was a big possibility, but that I would lose, not having done my best in the bout.

Also, some of the competitors were much bigger, stronger, and dare I say—better than me. I would employ psychological games to unsettle an opponent, and I think they worked because they would wonder why I would act the way I did, or say the things that I would say to them. They could not work out if I was totally fearless, or completely mad.

I knew what I was doing, however, I had decided that, before the fight, that it was going to end one way or the other. I was not interested in collecting trophies, as some of the competitors seemed to be.

I was more interested in doing my absolute best, showing the skills I possessed, and using them to devastating effect. Of course, I had to mix the styles back then, because Wing Chun in particular is a style that, for most tournaments, had almost 70% of its moves banned, because they were considered far too dangerous.

Use sparring practise, and tournament practise to hone your skills.
That is all it is for.

If you are focussed on collecting a trophy, the experience is largely a waste of time. I would say that you should focus on each individual bout. Nothing else really matters.

I was helpfully informed by my instructor, prior to my first ever bout, in 1993, that I would 'either win or lose', but just to let the 'natural course of events take place'. Further to that, if I were better than my opponent, I would prevail. But in no way was I do push it, because that would require more thinking and planning than the time during a fight allows.

That was excellent instruction too, because you really do not have time to *think*, only to *do*. Be instinctive, and trust those instincts. They have pretty much always worked for me.

Closing chapter notes: *I would like to thank you for sticking to this book right up until the end. For those who think I have not talked enough or in depth on certain aspects, I will expand on all the key Arts and styles mentioned in this book, in future books. This book was written to capture the essence of martial arts, the very things I feel are important for martial artists to know now.*

For now, I believe it is time to conclude this book on the essence of martial arts.

A final word: *Train hard, train safe and adopt a winning stance in everything you do. Act with respect and humility when dealing with others, and strive to be the best person, and the best martial artist you can be.*

Acknowledgements to my other Teachers

The following instructors have taught me in various styles over the years. It is appropriate here that I pay tribute to them. I am sure I will not be the last student to benefit from their expertise.

Sensei Eugene Codrington- Wado Ryu Karate Instructor from 1993-2000

Known in many circles as 'the gentleman', Sensei Eugene Codrington certainly was a very nice guy and also a competent instructor. I found his Wado Ryu style very suitable for me, and picked it up pretty well. To some degree Karate, whatever style it is, is more simplistic and so easier to pick up than other Arts, but also, like most things became increasingly hard to master.

The Wado Ryu style, or 'way of peace' is a more faster, more upright style of fighting, and incorporated elements of Ju Jitsu, whereas Shotokan, which I studied first, has lower, more powerful stances.

He was a good instructor, and in those eight years I feel I learned a lot. It was only tuition via the group method though, and I think for that reason my progress in the style was slower than I would have liked. True, in the Shotokan style I had mostly group tuition, but still, Karate is Karate. It is fair to say I was possibly spoilt by being trained on a one-to-one basis. I feel in many ways this is the only way to truly learn. Anything else is severely limiting, even if you can train against a variety of opponents.

Sensei was an extremely able teacher. His classes were often at capacity and so getting his attention was somewhat difficult. This served to entrench my belief that group sessions have their limit. I found the Wado Ryu style more suitable for me than the Shotokan style which was my foundation style.

I was happy to move on after the year 2000, and decided becoming a fully fledged full-time instructor should be my aim.

Sensei Dave Starkey

An excellent instructor who helped me attain my 'San Dan'—my 3rd degree black belt in Karate in 2007.

Sifu Chen Lei-Chen Tai Chi / Jeet Kune Do Instructor

Although I don't see Master Chen that often, he has has a profound influence on me when it comes to Chen style Tai Chi. He is also younger than me by 8 years, but his knowledge is exceptional. Trained at the University of Beijing, Master Chen not only has an extremely good command of the English language, but also, perhaps less surprisingly a real 'master' in the sense of really understanding his Art.

Secondly, Master Chen instructed me in the art of Jeet Kune Do, the style devised by Bruce Lee. I found this an excellent style, derived as it is from Wing Chun style of Kung Fu. It is much more invasive, and as a fighting style suited me very well. I see Master Chen for tuition as and when I can, because he is as good at teaching Chen Tai Chi as he is Jeet Kune Do. He does not claim a lineage going all the way back to Bruce Lee and his senior students . . . and that has never bothered me one bit, because he knows the system, and can teach it to great effect.

Sifu Guo Jian Wei-Chen Tai Chi / Kung Fu Instructor

Master Guo is an extremely humble man. His students are of an awesome standard, and I count myself extremely lucky and fortunate to be counted amongst his illustrious disciples. Against him I foolishly used Karate while he completely undid me with his complete understanding of tai chi. I have no doubt he went easy on me. If not, would I be here today?

I was introduced to Master Guo in the south-western Chinese province of GuiZhou. As well as his humility I can tell he was a very impressive instructor of Tai Chi. His style is mainly the Chen style, and while he did impart some knowledge to me, I know, just as is the case with my students, that it was information that barely scratches the surface, and arguably, takes years to truly understand.

Although relatively young, he's an 'old school' type of teacher, similar to Miss Li. A lot of people think Tai Chi is rather easy, until they practise it. I expect Master Guo's teaching is very similar. I regret that to date I haven't spent nearly as much time as I would like so I could learn more from him.

His home province is known as the 'mountain' province (self explanatory really), and so the altitude, compared to other parts of China (or to compare with the United Kingdom) is rather high.

I found this particular aspect important when it came to sparring. I've always considered myself reasonably fit, but in sparring for basically a 'round' (three minutes), it became increasingly obvious to me that I was'nt just fighting a great master, but also, altitude, and heat. These are factors you cannot help in a fighting situation . . . there is no such thing as ideal conditions for fighting, but you cannot expect the dice to always roll your way.

Index